DA____
WAY

RECREATIONAL PATH GUIDE

THE
DALES
WAY

ANTHONY BURTON

Aurum Press · Ordnance Survey

Acknowledgements

The author and publishers wish to thank the following for permission to reproduce photographs: Trevor Croucher, pp. 2-3, 13, 14, 18-19, 23, 25, 26-7, 53, 54, 55-6, 59, 60, 64, 68-9, 71, 72, 74, 80, 82-3, 88, 92-3; Barry Stacey/Lightwork: pp. 16, 98-9, 100, 103, 104, 120-1, 127, 128, 130, 134-5; Yorkshire and Humberside Tourist Board: pp. 34-5; Bradford Economic Development Unit: pp. 44, 47; Cumbria Tourist Board, pp. 110, 124.

Title page: Grassington and the view down Wharfedale
Front cover: Starbotton, looking down Wharfedale towards Kettlewell (Trevor Croucher)

First published 1995 by Aurum Press Limited,
25 Bedford Avenue, London WC1B 3AT
in association with the Ordnance Survey
Reprinted with revisions 1998

A catalogue record for this book is available from the British Library.

ISBN 1 85410 314 8

Book design by Robert Updegraff
Printed and bound in Italy by Printers Srl Trento

CONTENTS

How to use this guide

This guide is in three parts:
- The introduction, historical background to the area and advice for walkers.
- The path itself, described in seven chapters, with maps opposite each route description. This part of the guide also includes information on places of interest as well as a number of related short circular walks. Key sites are numbered in the text and on the maps to make it easy to follow the route description.
- The last part includes useful information such as local transport, accommodation, organisations involved with the path, and further reading.

The maps have been prepared by the Ordnance Survey for this guide using 1:25 000 Pathfinder maps as a base. The line of the Dales Way is shown in yellow, with the status of each section of the path – footpath or bridleway for example – shown in green underneath (see key on inside front cover). These rights of way markings also indicate the precise alignment of the path at the time of the original surveys, but in some cases the yellow line on these maps may show a route which is different from that shown by those older surveys, and in such cases walkers are recommended to follow the yellow route in this guide. Any parts of the path that may be difficult to follow on the ground are clearly highlighted in the route description, and important points to watch for are marked with letters in each chapter, both in the text and on the maps. *Some maps start on a right-hand page and continue on the left-hand page – black arrows (➡) at the edge of the maps indicate the start point.* Should there have been a need to alter the route since publication of this guide for any reason, walkers are advised to follow the waymarks or signs which have been put up on site to indicate this.

DISTANCE CHECKLIST

This list will help you in calculating the distances between places on the Dales Way, whether you are planning your overnight stays, or checking your progress.

Location	Approximate distance from previous location	
	miles	*km*
Leeds (Marsden monument)	0	0
Eccup	5.6	9.0
Menston	8.4	13.5
Ilkley Old Bridge	5.6	9.0
Bolton Abbey	5.6	9.0
Barden Bridge	3.4	5.5
Burnsall	3.4	5.5
Grassington	3.7	6.0
Kettlewell	6.2	10.0
Buckden Bridge	3.7	6.0
Hubberholme	1.2	2.0
Yockenthwaite	1.6	2.5
Cam Houses	6.3	10.2
Holme Hill (Gearstones)	3.0	4.8
Dent Head Viaduct	3.1	5.0
Dent (Church Bridge)	6.2	10.0
Millthrop	5.1	8.3
Lincoln's Inn Bridge	3.4	5.4
Crook of Lune Bridge	3.3	5.3
Burneside	8.2	13.2
Bowness	9.6	15.5

INTRODUCTION

The landscape of the Dales Way

The scenery along the Dales Way is every bit as grand as one would expect from a path that runs from one side of a great national park to the other, and then ends in a second national park. The beauty of the walk is that it allows one to enjoy this scenery in its full variety. It begins in the gritstone region that incorporates Yorkshire's best-known moor, that of Ilkley, a brooding area of dark stone, ruling the edge of the land like the black border on Victorian funeral notepaper. Coming down from the moor to the river valley, one moves westward and the land begins to lighten as the gritstone gives way to pallid limestone. Happily, the Way does not stay permanently on the valley floor, but brings a brief but glorious excursion to the uplands, where stunted hawthorn trees, bowed by the wind, cling tenaciously to cracks in the limestone pavement. The wild upland is in contrast to the tamed valley, which is green and fertile, and divided by stone walls. As one goes up-river, the Wharfe is constantly diminishing as it becomes first a stream, then little more than a trickle of springs, until its character is lost in the loneliest and bleakest part of the whole Way. Some find the wide expanses of Oughtershaw Moss intimidating; others glory in the space and freedom. And there is the satisfaction of overcoming the most difficult terrain of the whole walk – the dips and rises and peaty streams of Blea Moor. The reward for this effort is the walk down Dentdale, one of the most beautiful and peaceful of all the dales. The grand finale arrives with a walk in the shadow of the Howgill Fells with the mountains of Lakeland up ahead.

Some long-distance walks offer higher mountains and wilder scenery than the Dales; others boast high cliffs and coastal paths; there are also the gentler pleasures of hill and woodland and neat farms found along paths such as the Cotswold Way and the Ridgeway. But few walks, if any, offer such rich variety as the Dales Way. Here, there really is something for everyone – and anyone who arrives at the far end having found nothing to enjoy had probably better give up walking altogether.

THE GEOLOGY OF THE DALES

The Yorkshire Dales National Park, through which the Dales Way runs, is an area of great natural beauty and also one with a very specific character. And that character depends on the underlying rocks. Some 300 million years ago, the area was covered by a warm, shallow sea that supported an immense population of shellfish. Over the millenia, their hard outer cases built up and were compacted to form limestone. By the time the seas finally retreated, the heart of what we now call the Yorkshire Dales was one giant slab, 800 feet thick, known as Great Scar Limestone. It is not quite uniform, for in those ancient seas, reefs and submarine hills built up, appearing today as rocky outcrops and isolated hills. The limestone is also cut by deep vertical planes, through some of which material has been forced up from deep in the earth's core to create the veins of mineral ore that were eventually to be mined.

Waterfalls often rely on drainage from the hills and can be reduced to a mere trickle in dry weather.

Limestone pavements can be seen along the Way between Grassington and Kettlewell, and above Hubberholme.

It is the limestone of the Dales that has created the scenery so characteristic of this region. Over the aeons, many changes have occurred. Rivers have formed and eaten down through the rock to create valleys, but the most potent force in the creation of the modern landscape has been ice. A great Ice Age began around 100,000 years ago and lasted for over 80,000 years. Huge glaciers, perhaps as much as a thousand feet thick, covered the region at one time, their slow relentless movement wiping the rock clean. In time, the melting ice broke up the surface to create soil, scooping out smooth-sided valleys, of which Wharfedale is typical. But in places, the rock was left bare, creating limestone pavements such as those between Grassington and Kettlewell. And the rock was never a completely solid slab, but was formed into layers, which rivers eroded, creating small waterfalls such as those at Yockenthwaite. Elsewhere holes and caves formed, enabling rivers and streams to disappear and reappear in bewildering fashion.

To the east of the region was a delta, where a river met the sea that created the limestone. Here, sand was laid down, and this too was compressed to form the dark sandstone known as millstone grit. This hard stone is not easily worn away; even a busy river makes little impression. The Wharfe found a weak spot in the stone in the area we call The Strid, but even here it could only force a narrow channel. Elsewhere the softer shales have been eaten away, leaving the typical hard straight edge to heather moorland, seen at Otley Chevin and in the rocks of Ilkley. In the west, exactly the opposite geological formation is to be found in the Dent Fault. Here it is not deposition from above, but movement in the earth's surface which has allowed older, deeper rocks to push up through the crust. A walk down the Dales Way therefore incorporates three different regions, whose character was formed literally hundreds of millions of years ago.

It is not necessary to know the first thing about geology to appreciate the scenery of the Dales and the Lakes, but a basic knowledge will alert you to the changes that occur as you move from one area to the next. The hard solid gritstone provides few chances for water to escape, so that the ground easily becomes waterlogged. The typical top surface is peat, supporting heather and bilberry and, in the deeper areas, sphagnum and cotton grass. The soil in the limestone country is thin and acid – hence the numerous lime kilns providing lime as a fertiliser. Grasses thrive, notably sheep's fescue, creating a totally different environment to the gritstone areas. One of the most dramatic changes along the Dales Way is between the springy turf of the limestone uplands and the squelching peat of the moor.

WALKING THE DALES WAY

There are a few points to be made about the description of the Dales Way that now follows. Firstly, as the reader will soon realise, it is written from the point of view of someone walking in spring or summer. It is then that the trees are in leaf, the meadows bright with flowers and the bird population at its busiest and most songful. But each season brings its own delights. Some of my happiest childhood memories are of walking the dales and hills in the winter snow. Obviously, in the more exposed areas, one has to be prepared for bad weather, but the eerie, muffled solitude can be exhilarating. If you look at more than one guide to, or map of, the Dales Way, you will soon discover that no one seems to agree on just how long it is. Some guide books

The black-faced Swaledale ram, with its spectacular horns, is the symbol of the National Park.

assume that the walker will be turning off the official path, to visit Dent or Sedbergh, for example. The distances quoted here do not allow for such detours. However, diversions have been suggested in the form of circular walks off the Way itself. These have been selected to help the walker experience all the variety that the scenery has to offer. Often this means that where the main walk stays in the valley, the circular walk will take to the hills. Or, as at Grassington, the walk may be chosen to provide a view of an important element of the local scenery. In many respects the Dales Way is the ideal introduction to long-distance walking, offering a tremendous variety of scenery from riverside meadows to windswept peaty moorland. Given the nature of the terrain, it is surprisingly undemanding for, although it climbs to a height of around 1,500 feet when crossing the watershed between Wharfedale and Dentdale, its gradients are quite gentle. The walk is demanding enough, however, to give a real sense of achievement when the end is reached.

The first question to be decided is the starting point. Many walkers still regard the true Dales Way as being the section between Ilkley and Bowness, with the Leeds to Ilkley section as a tacked-on extra. Then there is the question of which direction to go in. Most people prefer to walk from east to west, perhaps feeling that the Dales Way should start in the Dales and not in the Lake District. Yet there is a case for going the other way, particularly in summer. Accommodation in some of the remoter areas is not always easy to come by, and those few starting from Bowness will not be competing for beds with the more numer-ous parties going in the opposite direction. This guide, however, goes with the majority and begins the walk in Leeds.

As with all long-distance walks, there is a lot to be said for good advance planning, particularly when it comes to accommodation. There are five youth hostels on or close to the route: Linton, Kettlewell, Dentdale, Kendal and Windermere, but other accommo-dation is limited. Villages are few and far between, and there are long sections in which only isolated farms are met. Fortunately, many of these do bed and breakfast, and may provide an evening meal as well. In the busy summer months it will be necessary to book in advance, and in order to do this, one should have some idea of how far one can walk in a day. A good rule is to aim to do less than you think you can manage, and never more. If you arrive too early at a stopover, there will always be attractive countryside to explore. It is also essential to bear in mind that the walking is not uniform and the weather may vary. It is therefore common sense to assume less than perfect conditions. Another factor to allow for is that there are long

Sun breaking through storm clouds brings drama to the Dales landscape near

Grassington.

sections with no pub, café or shop, so you will need to take food and, more importantly, drink with you. Waterproof clothing is also essential, as are good-quality walking boots. Sunburn can be every bit as unpleasant as a thorough soaking and, if you know you are going to be out in the sun all day, it is a good idea to wear a hat. Finally, there are two sections of the Dales Way that present potential difficulties: the high-level walk from Grassington to Kettlewell and the trek across the watershed. Here, cloud could come right down over the tops, reducing visibility to a few feet, in which case an instruction such as 'head for the tree on the brow of the hill' will not be much use. In these circumstances, a compass becomes an invaluable aid. But that alone is not enough – you have to know how to use it in conjunction with the map. Always make sure that someone knows you are out walking and expected at a certain place at a certain time. And if you are alone, then help will get to you quicker if you assist the helpers – a good blast on a whistle can save a lot of waiting.

Having covered the gloomy side of walking, it is perhaps as well to stress that this is a wonderfully enjoyable walk, which many, many people do every year without problem or mishap. The entire route between Leeds and Bowness can be accomplished by most reasonably fit people in a week. For the shorter route from Ilkley, five and a half days is a reasonable timetable. But this is a walk that encourages lingering, simply because there is so much to enjoy. One can only sympathise with one walker who, having got to the end, rang the office to say he was taking an extra week off, turned round and did it all over again.

WILDLIFE

For much of its length, the Dales Way is seldom far from a riverbank, and no walker could fail to be aware of the busy bird population that the rivers support. On the water itself the ubiquitous mallard is the main inhabitant, sometimes joined by moorhen. Occasionally one is lucky enough to spot rarer visitors, such as a pair of goosander. Keeping guard over the bank is the solitary heron; at the approach of the walker it will usually fly ahead with a huge flap of its wide wings and take up its stance again further on. The rocks that poke through so many of the Dales rivers are ideal perches for some of the most attractive birds to be seen along the way. There are the little brown and white dippers, and also wagtails, particularly the pied and yellow varieties. We associate gulls with the sea, but black-headed gulls are very much residents of river and estuary, as are martins and swallows, which zoom in, feeding on the clouds of insects that hover over the water. And one may well catch sight of the kingfisher, unmistakable and unforgettable in its brilliant plumage.

The uplands have their own residents, some of which can be heard even when they are not seen. The air echoes to the song of the skylark, the wonderfully evocative cry of the peewit, and the harsher sound of the grouse. In amongst these, the sweet song of the meadow pipit might be overheard. This little brown bird is unremarkable in itself, yet it is perhaps the commonest of all the upland birds.

Woodland is a feature of the walk, offering shelter and food to a wide variety of birds from woodpeckers, nuthatch and tits to the familiar wood pigeon. The pheasant was introduced to Britain from eastern Europe and China, but it has been with us since Norman times and now seems a native species. It is regularly seen, and even more often heard, in many of the woods and copses. Birds of prey are surprisingly scarce, and even the kestrel, one of the more familiar, is rare along the walk. Birds, however, are not the only form of wildlife to take to the wing. The meadows of the valley bottoms are home to a huge range of insects, including many varieties of butterfly. Strid Wood is also noted for its butterfly population.

Wild animals are, inevitably, seen less frequently than birds, although rabbits can be met almost anywhere along the way. The nocturnal badger and the otter are more elusive, but there is a very good chance of spotting weasels and stoats. There are also deer in the woods, but one has to be patient and quiet to see them. The Wharfe is a trout river – and even if you never see a single trout you will certainly see the fly fishermen trying to tempt them into view. Roach, dace, grayling and barbel are all found in the rivers and streams.

DALES RAILWAYS

The Dales were not an obviously attractive area for railway builders, offering a daunting procession of hills and deep valleys, and few large towns to provide customers.

The first line encountered along the Way is seen only in the distance. At the point of crossing, it is far underground in the two-mile-long Bramhope Tunnel, part of the line from Leeds to Thirsk, which was opened in 1848. Nearly 2,000 men were needed to build the tunnel and not everyone survived the hard, dangerous work. A memorial in Otley churchyard, in the form of a miniature Bramhope Tunnel, is a witness to the navvies who died.

Although the nineteenth-century railway companies were often in competition, they sometimes co-operated. The North Eastern built a branch line to Otley, and then joined the Midland to extend it to Ilkley. It was later extended again to Skipton. This line suffered a mixed fate. The Otley branch is closed, but the Ilkley branch was extended south to Shipley and survives, while that to Skipton was also closed. Part of the latter has reopened at Embsay as a steam railway and work is going ahead to push the line forward as far as the old Bolton Abbey station. Soon the sound of the steam whistle will echo over the Dales Way. In 1902 there was a somewhat forlorn attempt to bring rails into the heart of the Dales, with a branch from Embsay to Grassington. Passenger services were closed down in 1930, but the line continues as a freight service from quarries south of Grassington.

The central section of the Dales appeared intractable and looked as if it would also prove unprofitable, so it was left alone. Over to the west, however, the railway builders came up with a route which rational analysis suggested would turn out to be equally unprofitable – the Settle and Carlisle Railway. It was never a sensible project. The Midland Railway wanted a route to the north and railway politics prevented them from entering into deals with other companies. One of the best-known lines in Britain, the Settle–Carlisle was one of the most difficult to build. In places it ran through bogs that were so soft that wheelbarrows used barrels for wheels to prevent them from sinking. In other spots, the dried-up clay was so hard it could only be shifted by blasting.

Only one line could have challenged the Settle–Carlisle for the railway drama award: the route from Ingleton to Penrith. Built in the 1840s, it should have been part of a through-route running all the way from Skipton to Scotland. However, it got stuck at Ingleton, the promoters having run out of money. This was bad news for the Lancaster and Carlisle Railway, begun in 1844 under the great engineer Joseph Locke. The company decided that if the line from Skipton was not going to get to them, they would go and meet it. In 1857 work began on a route from their main line at Low Gill, down to Ingleton. But railway politics denied it main-line status; by the time it was completed, the Lancaster and Carlisle had been absorbed into a different system, which still survives as part of the main West Coast line from London to Scotland, while the Ingleton route was doomed to languish as a branch line until its closure. But what a superb branch line it must have been.

The branch line to Windermere completes a splendid array of routes that tackled and conquered the Pennine Hills.

Chamber End Fold, one of the little cobbled lanes that run off Grassington High Street.

OLD WAYS AND TRACKS

It is not possible to locate prehistoric roads or trackways in the Dales with any degree of accuracy. All one can say with certainty is that during the Bronze Age, from around 2,000 to 500 BC, there were settlements in the Ilkley area, for the people of the time left their distinctive carvings on the stones. The other recognisable early marks along the Way are the 'Celtic' fields and settlements around Grassington. With the coming of the Romans, however, there is firm evidence of road building.

A Roman road led out from York to an auxiliary fort at Ilkley, and on the path near Ilkley modern walkers are following in the steps of the legions. If, however, you want clearer physical evidence of the work of Roman engineers, you have to move on to the west and the Cam High Road. This ran from Bainbridge to Ingleton and is now part green way, part footpath and part modern road. The Dales Way follows the old road from the point where it joins the Pennine Way near Cam Houses to Gearstones, where the modern Ingleton road takes over the line set down by the Romans. Walking the route today one can still see that the way was once paved, but was this the work of Romans? It is impossible to say, for this route has been used for many, many generations by drovers and carriers.

The Dark Ages are as little known as the prehistoric period, but by medieval times, patterns once again become clear. The abbeys and priories were great landowners, whose estates stretched over many miles. Fountains Abbey, near Ripon, was amongst the wealthiest and most powerful in Britain – which is ironic, since it was founded by ascetics who found monastic life in York too luxurious. The main connecting link between the abbey and the distant farms was Mastiles Lane, which ran across Malham Moor to cross the Wharfe at Kilnsey, before heading off for Pateley Bridge. It can still be seen as a green way crawling up the hill above Kilnsey. Other 'roads' were used for the busy movement of goods carried on pack animals and for driving sheep, cattle and geese to market. Some were even given a name: Bycliffe Road, for example, which crosses the Dales Way between Grassington and Kettlewell, heading down to Conistone. A feature of many of these early tracks is the way in which they lead straight up over the hills, as resolutely as Roman roads. The reason is simple: they were not designed for wheeled vehicles, hence the old narrow, high-arched packhorse bridges, with low parapets to allow room for the panniers on the animals' backs. Specialist roads were also constructed, such as those leading to mines; 'Coal Road' in Dentdale is

The seventeenth-century bridge across the Wharfe at Burnsall shows how well the hard local gritstone survives weathering and floods.

one that still keeps its old name. Then there were the great wide drove roads, which kept to open country. By the end of the seventeenth century, literally thousands of head of cattle were being brought down from Scotland to be fattened on rich southern pastures and then sold. There were staging posts along the way, where the drovers met, and one of the most important was at Gearstones. There is now little if anything to show that there was a market here every week until 1870.

The eighteenth century saw a great spate of road building by turnpike trusts, who recouped their costs by charging tolls. They had certain obligations to meet in return, which included providing milestones, a few of which still survive. In time, when the local authorities took over the road, they installed their own, and many of their distinctive cast-iron milestones can be seen today. There are, however, one or two of the older stone variety still to be found along the Dales Way.

This fence was built to prevent snow sliding down and blocking the Settle

and Carlisle Railway as it crosses the head of Dentdale.

FARMING IN THE DALES

Farmers have done more than anyone else to create the landscape of the Dales. The old pattern of farming existed for many centuries, and was a logical use of natural resources, working with the land and the rhythm of the seasons. The typical dale has three distinct regions: the lush and fertile valley, the lower flanks of the hills, which provide rough pasture, and the high fells and moors. In such a landscape crop-growing has to take second place to stock-rearing.

Down on the valley floor rich meadows provide the hay for winter feeding. A striking feature of the land is the pattern of small fields, sometimes with a stone barn in every field. These barns were built not just for storage, but also as byres. The hay is forked up to the loft, and can be dropped down to the byre, where perhaps four or five cows have their winter quarters. The manure goes back out into the field to enrich it for the next season's growth. It is an efficient system and, as a side product, ensures that on the few remaining farms that keep to the old ways, the meadows are rich with herbs and flowers. Meadow management is the key to success. In spring, cattle and the ewes with their young lambs feed in the valley fields. Then they are moved up the slopes, and the fields are left to grow until haymaking time. The cattle never move further than the lower slopes, but the sheep roam far over the fells. The black-faced Swaledales are so typical of the region that they have been chosen as the symbol for the Dales National Park.

Another typical feature of the Dales are the stone walls that are found throughout the region. In the valley bottoms they form an intricate pattern defining individual fields, while on the steep sides and the higher ground they stretch away in straight lines. Much of the stone from which they are built came from the process of clearing the land. On occasions the presence of a good supply of stone would make it easier to set a wall on one line rather than another, hence some of the bizarre shapes and extravagant curves that appear. The walls of the Dales are often referred to as drystone walls, as they are built without cement or mortar; if such a wall is to stand then it must be constructed with considerable skill. First the stone is collected on the site, and the line of the wall laid down. A trench, generally around four feet wide, is dug until a good solid base is reached. Two rows of large, more or less square, boulders are then laid, with their roughest sides facing inwards. The space between is filled with small, irregular stones and fragments. Even these are not just casually thrown in, but arranged to leave as few spaces as possible. It is on the solidity of these footings that the strength of the wall will depend. Now the wall is built up, each successive layer being a little shorter than the last, so that it narrows towards the top. Each layer must sit well on the one below, and should be well packed with fillings. 'Throughs' are placed at regular intervals, running the full width of the wall to bind it together. The final touch comes when the coping stones are laid to give the wall a clean, regular top. Careful selection of the right stone for the right job is essential throughout the whole process.

The walls require numerous openings. Gateways are the most obvious but are not the only ones to be seen. There are also 'cripple holes', low, square openings that allow sheep through the wall but not cattle. Stiles are created by leaving a gap in the wall, slightly wider at the top than at the bottom, allowing humans to pass, but keeping the sheep out. Simple stony stepladders are also common. The stone wall comes quite literally from the land on which it stands, so it is not surprising that with the passage of years it seems more like a natural than a man-made feature.

Although the landscape of the Dales may appear to have a time-less quality, modern farming methods have brought about consider-able changes. The farmer who wants to increase his herd has either to buy in winter feed or boost the yield of the meadows with artificial fer-tilisers. In either case the decision will have important effects on the land. When food is brought in, there is less need to keep to the strict seasonal pattern of grazing and harvesting. The use of fertilisers may increase grass yields, but leads to an impoverishment of the meadow flowers. This change is reflected, too, in the number of derelict field barns seen throughout the area. Some old fields have gone for ever beneath new conifer plantations; for example, on the walk through the woods in Dentdale, one comes across a forlorn little barn aban-doned in the gloom of regimented trees.

It is easy to think of the Dales landscape as 'natural' and 'wild', yet it is as much the creation of the farmer and his flocks as is the meadow in the valley bottom. Areas such as Dentdale with a narrow valley floor impose limitations on the size of herds, and thus on the size of farms. Elsewhere, a wide valley floor can take bigger herds. Which, incidentally, is why broad-bottomed Wensleydale is a centre of cheese-making. Walkers who admire the unique landscape of the Dales should drink a toast to the long generations of farmers who have produced it.

THE
DALES
WAY

1 LEEDS TO ILKLEY OLD BRIDGE

via Bramhope and Menston   *19 miles (30.5 km)*

The Dales Way officially runs from Ilkley to Bowness, but when the Ramblers' Association of the West Riding first mooted this long-distance path they thought in terms of a walk from Leeds, and the Leeds-Ilkley Link was eventually added. The advantage of including this section is that it has a character quite unlike that found anywhere else along the route; the disadvantage is that it represents a long first leg, and, as it nears Ilkley, quite a demanding one. It is possible to break the journey, most conveniently as far as accommodation is concerned, at Otley.

The walk starts at the Marsden monument **1** at the southern tip of Woodhouse Moor, officially known as Hyde Park, close to the university. H.R. Marsden was one of those bewhiskered Victorian dignitaries whose claim to fame has long been forgotten, but who inspired other worthies to set up his statue in 1878. Queen Victoria, across the road, does not seem to disapprove. Woodhouse Moor itself is a green finger pushing down into the city centre, an open space used for generations for meetings and fairs. It had its one moment in the historic limelight in 1643 when General Sir Thomas Fairfax gathered his Parliamentary forces for the successful attack on the Royalist army holding Leeds. Today this part of the old moor is little more than a narrow strip of grassland, but it does provide an open space for the walk out of Leeds. This walk goes up the side of the green along Raglan Road, passing Harrisons Almshouses, whose rather grim exterior hides a more pleasant interior, where the little houses face onto a grassy courtyard. Turn right at the road junction **A** into Rampart Road and carry straight on along Delph Lane. This is very much a red-brick area with Victorian terraces (some of which with their high steps are really quite elegant), as well as rather grander villas. As you get closer to the top of the ridge, so brick gives way to more prestigious stone, the soot-blackened sandstone that lends houses of this type an air of rather sombre dignity. The road comes to an end quite dramatically at Woodhouse Cliff **B**.

One of the great surprises of the walk out of Leeds is to find that for most of the way the path is almost rural. Here the land drops away very steeply – too steep for housing, so it has been left as woodland.

Turn left onto the upper-level footpath. To the left, a high stone wall keeps the houses out of sight, while the path itself runs through mature woods, brightened by rhododendrons. There are glimpses between the trees of urban Leeds far below, and the noise of traffic means that you are always reminded of its presence, but it remains a pleasant walk, very popular with the locals. One of the houses, at least, takes in the view with an oriel window peering over the high wall. Where the wall begins to turn to the left, continue straight ahead on the middle of the three paths. For a while it does really seem like a country lane, bordered by trees, but it soon emerges to run round the backs of the houses, eventually arriving at the main road.

Cross over the road and go down the lane signposted 'Public Footpath: Meanwood Valley Trail'. This is an area of contrasts. To the left are traditional stone villas, to the right a modern development of flats, looking rather as if they have been built from a giant Lego kit, while the walk itself goes down a green valley with a small stream

The Black Prince looks out over City Square in the centre of Leeds.

alongside the path, and a pond with water lilies. At the road crossing carry on in the same direction down Highbury Road towards the mill chimney, a handsome landmark with its bricks and iron bands all freshly painted. At the mill **C** turn left on a cobbled lane that runs past the mill pond, then right down the narrow lane, passing through an area of allotments. At the wooden stile continue on past the cricket field on the right, and just beyond the field turn right at the little bridge that crosses the mill stream with its sluice gates. Follow the path as it snakes round to the left. Turn left to take the paved pathway into the park, passing a children's playground on the way. Cross the stream by the packhorse bridge above a small weir. It is obvious that at one time there were a number of mills supported by this one stream, for weirs and paddle gear crop up all along the way. Follow the path round to the left to an attractive row of eighteenth-century stone cottages, Hustlers Row **D**. Cross over the footbridge with the wooden railings and then turn immediately right, between the stone gateposts, onto the track marked with a yellow arrow.

This now becomes a very delightful and seemingly wholly rural walk. The footpath follows the line of an old mill leat surrounded by woodland. Where mill leat and natural stream unite at the weir, cross the bridge on the right and continue following the line of the stream. Turn right almost immediately and then left to leave the woods by a wooden gate, and continue along the path by the fence. It is still pleasant walking through fields, with the woods on the left, but up ahead the noise of traffic becomes ever more intrusive. The path follows a little stream and eventually arrives at a road. Turn left, cross the road and follow it up towards the busy Leeds ring road. Just before reaching the main road **E**, turn right onto the footpath. A high hawthorn hedge, through which a straggle of dog roses have fought their way, forms an attractive visual screen – but not, alas, an aural one. Even so, it comes as quite a surprise to find the tower blocks of Moortown looming up ahead. But this is the city asserting its presence for the last time. The path swings round to go under the ring road through a tunnel. When you reach the other side, turn right up the steps and take the surfaced path towards the wood. Cross the stile into the woods and you can really feel that Leeds has been left behind.

Keep to the path on the right, which runs close by the stream. Over to the left are the ruined remains of the former Scotland woollen mill **2**, with the watercourse and mounting for the wheel still visible. This is a walk through mature broad-leaved woodland, although the ruined stone houses are a reminder of the old industrial days. The woods are overgrown and tangled, so that the sound of traffic is very

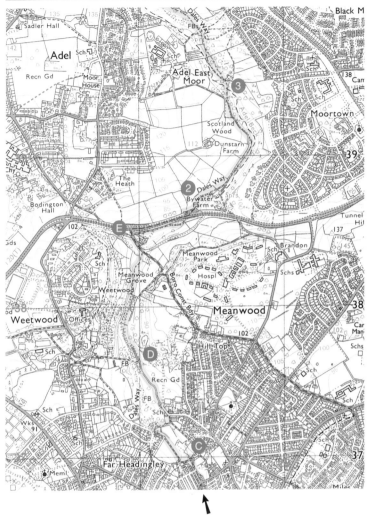

quickly killed and only the birdsong remains. At first the path follows the stone wall at the lip of the valley but, where the way divides, keep to the right beside the seven stone arches of the aqueduct that carries water from Eccup Reservoir to Leeds **3**. Turn left onto the higher of the two tracks, which continues as a high-level route through a jumble of sandstone boulders. The way is marked by yellow arrows. The path crosses a hill stream, passing over a stone step and on to a small round pond and a spring which is known by the curious name of The Slabbering Baby, referring to the carved head on the fountain. Take the path going uphill to the right along the edge of a particularly attractive area of woodland, where the pale-silver birch contrasts with the darker shades of oak. At the broad sandy track **F** turn left; just out of sight but only a few yards from the track are the grotesque weathered rocks of Adel Crag. The broad track comes out at the car park by the road. Cross over the road and go straight on along the same track to leave the woods by the wooden stile. Turn right and follow the path around the edge of the field.

After the enclosed woods, the walker is now in open country with expansive views. The path runs through an area of scrubby woodland at the side of a golf course, so keep an eye open for missiles. Cross over the road and take the track to the right of the house. The path continues along the fence at the edge of the golf course before reaching typical pasture farmland, very open apart from a few patches of trees. At the corner of the field turn left over the stile and head for the left-hand edge of the line of conifers that mark the position of Eccup Reservoir. There is just the barest glimpse of water through gaps in the trees. From the reservoir take the path down by the side of the hedge and turn right onto the road. This leads down to a small bridge over a stream, which swarms with trout – no doubt escapees from the reservoir. At this point **G** the road divides: turn first left then right at the road junction by the farm. Leave the road on the footpath by the farm, and after the farmyard turn left to head for the stile in the corner of the field and right over the stile by the gate. Continue following the rutted farm track across the fields. This is airy upland country, whose chief inhabitants appear to be flocks of peewits, their delicate cry sometimes interrupted by the harsh note of a pheasant. Continue following the track as it veers off to follow the line of the field to the left. At a stile **H** turn right along a fence bordered by a hawthorn hedge. As you top the gentle rise, the hills on the far side of Wharfedale come into view for the first time. Gradually the view widens to include Arthington church down in the valley and, on a good day, the North Yorkshire Moors. The path now goes straight downhill over a series of stiles to a broad track **I**. Turn left onto the track as it passes between the farmhouse and the barns. Now the view extends over the Wharfedale Viaduct, carrying the railway from Leeds to Harrogate; beyond this can be seen the isolated rocky outcrop of Almscliff Crag.

The line of the walk has now changed to run along the southern rim of the Wharfedale valley as a green lane with a bank on one side and a stone wall on the other. It is known, aptly, as Bank Top Lane, and is soon climbing steadily uphill. Cross over the road and go through the kissing gate to follow the line of the fence in the direction signposted 'Ebor Way'. Over to the right is a large working quarry. At

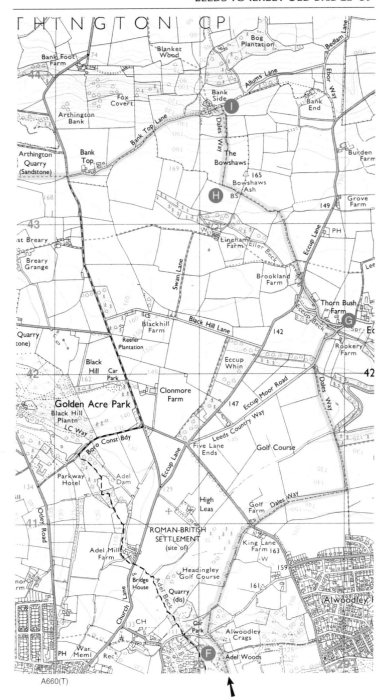

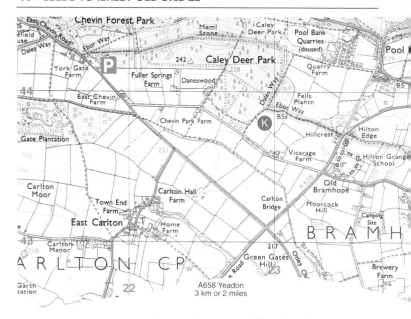

the next iron gate follow the fence round to the left, cross a stile in the fence on the left and immediately turn right over a second stile. Carry on in the same direction along the line of the tall hedge. Look out for a stile in the hedge on the right, cross over and follow the lane down to the road, past a small pond. Countryside now gives way to suburbia, though suburbia of the more expensive variety; one house appears to have strayed from the set of *Gone with the Wind*. This is now the outskirts of the dormitory suburb of Bramhope. Cross straight over the main road and go up Breary Lane – which is actually running over Bramhope railway tunnel. At the crossroads by the elaborate wrought-iron signpost with its lantern perched on top, there are a number of shops and a pub. Cross straight over and go down Old Lane. When the houses finally come to an end J turn right, doubtless with no sense of reluctance whatsoever, onto the footpath leading to Pool Bank. It is a curiosity that the walk through Bramhope should be so less interesting – and so less rural – than the far longer walk out of Leeds.

The path goes round to the left and again offers superb views over towards Almscliff Crag. Cross a stile and follow the path along the side of a somewhat tumbledown stone wall. At a break in the wall, turn diagonally to the right towards the stile by the gatepost. The sense of being quite high above the valley floor and near the summit of the hills is reinforced by the path, where the thin soil has been

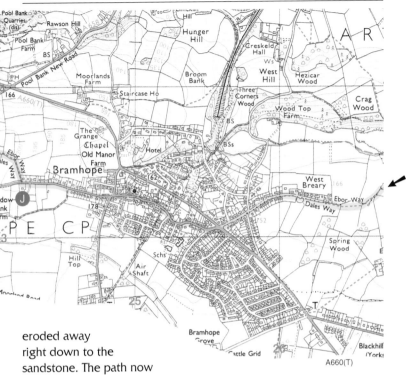

eroded away
right down to the
sandstone. The path now
leads down by the side of a wall and
then, as it nears the road, is squashed in between a wall and a tall
hedge. Cross over the road at the top of Pool Bank (not easy in the
heavy traffic) and carry straight on in the same direction on the footpath beside the houses, signposted 'Ebor Way'. There is a brief,
unsavoury interlude as the track passes a large rubbish tip, then a
return to the upland fields and the cry of the curlew. The birds seem
surprisingly unconcerned by human intruders, hovering and landing
quite close to walkers. Cross a stile to take the path that runs along
the top of a patch of deciduous woodland, and then turn right **K** onto
the wide sandy track running downhill along the edge of the conifer
plantation. Follow this right down to the edge of the wood and, just
before the stile at the iron gate, turn left onto another sandy track
which continues on through the plantation for about a mile.

Turn right at the road and, after about 300 yards, turn left at the
second of two footpaths, signposted to West Chevin Road. It begins
as a tarmac path, but soon becomes a stony track, running along the
lip of the valley. Where the broad track swings round to the left, carry
straight on as the path reaches an area of, literally, high drama. To the

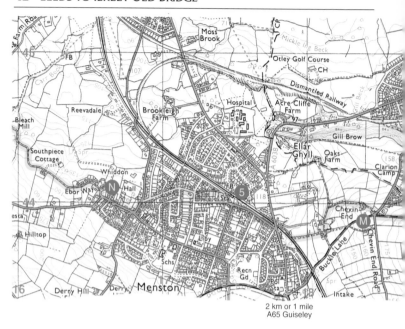

2 km or 1 mile
A65 Guiseley

left is cultivated land, with a pub visible, and approachable, across the fields, but the route itself goes through coarse grassland. Heather, bilberry and gorse are mingled with the jagged outline of dark gritstone poking through at the escarpment edge. The views are as good as any on the Dales Way and a topograph **4** set among the rocks helps to identify the features. It genuinely is possible to see such contrasting symbols of different ages as the towers of York Minster and the transmission mast at Holme Moss. Having enjoyed the view, it is time to begin the descent to the valley. Scrub now appears, then patches of birch followed by some splendid mature beech. Gritstone crags seem to have burst through the land, scattering massive boulders before them. The path wanders along, roughly following the line of the wall. On reaching an area of particularly large boulders, you will see that the obvious path turns steeply downhill. To follow the Dales Way, however, turn left **L**, crossing a stile that leads into a field, and take the path across to the road.

The excitement is over for a while now as the Way keeps to the roads. Turn right onto the road, past large boarding kennels to a T-junction. Turn left and then right. At the road junction, cross over to the pub and take the footpath that goes through the car park **M**. Cross the farmyard to the stile in the corner and take the path along the wall down to another farm. Turn left onto the surfaced track and at the next

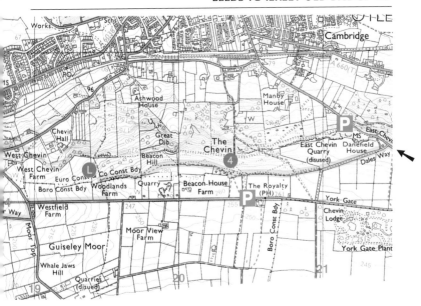

farmhouse turn right to cross a stile beside a high stone wall and join the obvious track. The path turns right when it reaches the railway, crosses a small stream via a footbridge and eventually joins the road. Cross over the bridge and the main road to go down Station Road to Menston Station **5**. This is a surprisingly busy line, recently electrified, that links Ilkley to Leeds and Bradford. It is possible to break the journey here, either staying in Menston itself or using the train to reach one of the other nearby towns. To continue on the walk, however, go past the station and turn right down Westbourne Drive. At the railway, turn left onto the path by the side of the wall that divides the walk from pristine suburban gardens. As the lane ends, carry straight on down Fairfax Road, which leads to the rather dour Victorian church. Turn left at the end of the road and then turn right at the crossroads. This is the older centre of Menston, with stone back-to-back terraces. Where the road turns sharply left, turn right onto the lane signposted 'Footpath to Burley Woodhead' **N**. The lane immediately goes round to the left.

The houses of Menston are now left behind, and this old mill lane offers a peaceful walk between hedgerows. The view opens up on the right over Wharfedale, but this is gentle, agricultural land with little hint of the craggy moorland not far away. The sound of water splashing over a weir indicates that this is the site of a mill, and the path soon reaches a mill pond, continuing up to the gateway of Bleach Mill

The large single block of The Calf sits below the gritstone outcrop of The Cow, together forming The Cow and Calf Rocks, Ilkley Moor.

House, then turning to the left of it, to become a narrow way running past the old mill building. Cross the stone stile at the end of the lane and follow the path beside the wall. Leave the farm buildings to your left and cross another stile by the wooden gate. Follow the line of the wall and go through an iron gate into a little lane leading to a row of old stone cottages. These are dated 1734, but the one with tiny square windows is probably older and others are certainly a little later. Go through the kissing gate at the end of the row **O** and continue straight across the field over a series of stiles, then turn left at the surfaced driveway that leads up to the road. Cross over the main road, turn right at the road junction then left by the Public Footpath sign **P**.

This is a remarkably sudden transformation. From a walk across fields to the busy traffic of a main road, a wooden gate opens straight onto rough moorland of bracken, peppered with patches of heather and bilberry. Take the upper of the two tracks that leads to the top of the line of crags. Then, at the rocks, where the track divides, turn right to follow the path along the top of the escarpment. This is typical grit-stone country, where the stone breaks through the valley rim in great square blocks like the work of some giant mason. Where the path divides continue following the edge on the right. The way now dips down into a deep ghyll with a small stream running down the middle, then climbs back again to meet up with the track above the crags. On one side, you will see heather moorland with small bogs sprouting tell-tale cotton grass, and on the other a steep bracken-covered slope leading down to farmland. Soon the area's most distinctive landmark comes into view: the crag and massive isolated boulder known as the Cow and Calf **6**. The path heads downhill through a jumble of stones and boulders to reach it.

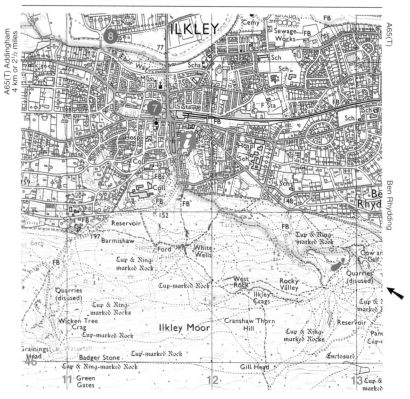

The top of the path is marked by a large stone outcrop, beyond which is a quarry whose near-vertical faces have been used by generations of rock climbers as a practice ground. There is a whole series of routes, each with its own name, although few now know where the names originated – who, for example, was Josephine who lent her name to one of the climbs? This is also the starting point for a circular walk over Ilkley Moor (see p. 48). The path now passes through a stand of conifers below a second, smaller quarry, then crosses a stream burbling down a steep rocky gully to flow into a little lake known simply as The Tarn. Join the path that runs round the edge and follow it down towards Ilkley.

This town grew up in the last century as a health resort, offering medicinal spring waters and hearty walks in the fresh air. There is still a feel of the prosperous spa town as one leaves the moor and walks down the broad, tree-lined street to the town centre. Visit the parish church of All Saints **7**, however, and a different, older story is told. At first glance this is a typical Victorian church, but details show a long history; the main south doorway has Norman 'dog-tooth' decoration, and inside – in the tower – are fragments of two Saxon crosses, carved with grotesque beasts and a rather crude, and very worn, Adam and Eve. Taking us further back in time are two pillars from a Roman temple, carved to show a priestess, or possibly a goddess, and altar vessels. The Roman connection can be pursued outside, where the square shape of the Roman fort of Olicana can still be traced on the ground. Ilkley's story is told in more detail in the local museum, housed in the rugged seventeenth-century manor house next to the church.

The 'official' route through Ilkley goes down Bridge Lane to the newer of the two bridges – not all that new, but an elegant iron span decorated with the Yorkshire rose. Turn left onto the riverside walk under an avenue of trees, past a hotel offering boats for hire. Immediately beyond that is the Old Bridge **8**, marking the end of the Leeds extension and the start of the main Dales Way. A sign announces, inaccurately, that there are just 73 miles left to go.

Flower beds and Victorian shop fronts are reminders that Ilkley developed as a spa town in the last century.

CIRCULAR WALK FROM THE COW AND CALF, ILKLEY

5 ½ miles (9 km)

From the top of the quarry at the Cow and Calf rocks **A**, take the path across the moor to the long line of crags known as Rocky Valley. The path crosses a stream and then turns down the valley. A line of conifers appears on the brow of the hill to the left; just before reaching them **B**, turn sharp left to take the track that doubles back up the hillside as a stony staircase. At the top of the hill, where the tracks cross **C**, continue straight on, turning away from Ilkley towards the open moorland.

High up on the moor the track leads into a marshy area where there has been serious erosion and duckboards have been laid to protect the damaged patches. The path levels out and the Twelve Apostles stone circle **9** appears on the left. There are eight stone circles on the moor, all dating from the Bronze Age, and this is the most impressive.

A sense of isolation is one of the attractions of this walk; often the only sounds are the call of the peewit and the bleat of sheep, yet this was once a busy enough thoroughfare to warrant a milestone telling travellers they are on track for Eldwick, Saltaire and Bingley **D**. At this milestone, turn off to the left on the narrow path marked by short white posts. It runs almost parallel to a stone wall on the right, but gradually converges with it. Instead of a stony path there is now turf on peat, surrounded by cotton grass. Nearing the wall, another white post indicates a turn to the right across a stone stile. Follow the path bearing away to the left, and head past the biggest of the boulders to return to the wall **E**. Here are a number of old boundary stones marked with the name Horncliffe Well. Cross the stone stile in the wall and follow the path beside the wire fence. A few deviations are necessary to avoid very boggy areas, easily recognised by the patches of cotton grass, and there are also marshy streams to cross. One soon arrives at a line of grouse butts, small pits with drystone walls in which the guns wait for the birds to appear over the horizon, pushed towards them by the beaters. The butts end at a ridge and a rock outcrop **F**. Over to the right what looks like a pile of gravel is a prehistoric cairn, known as the Great Skirtful of Stones.

Turn left onto the rutted track, as indicated by a footpath sign painted on the rocks. Where the track divides, turn right, crossing the stream to reach the bank of the reservoir. From here the path snakes through a rather boggy area towards a post clearly visible on the horizon. Beyond this yellow post, indicating the boundary of Ilkley Moor, the path becomes more distinct and heads off to a small crag **G**. Here, where the way divides, turn left towards a large flat rock, the Pancake Stone **10**. This has curious carvings: depressions surrounded by a doughnut-like ring, the so-called 'cup-and-ring' marks, which have been dated to the Bronze Age. Turn right at the stone to follow the path downhill and back to the Dales Way.

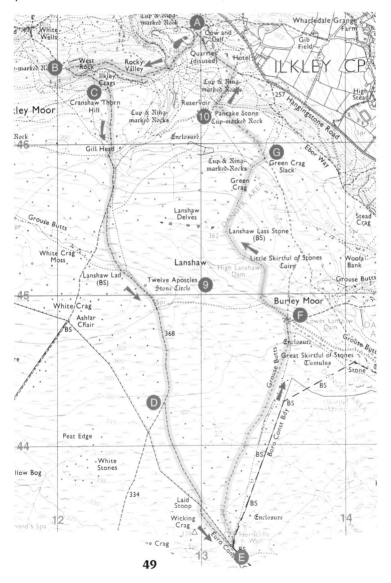

2 ILKLEY OLD BRIDGE TO GRASSINGTON

via Bolton Abbey and Burnsall   *16 miles (26 km)*

The Old Bridge is genuinely venerable, over three hundred years old, spanning the river with two stone arches. Climb up the steps to the bridge and continue on along the tarmacked path by the nursery, where a fine copper beech spreads its branches across the path. The river now swings away in an extravagant bend and the path goes straight on to join the minor road passing Ilkley's tennis and squash courts. Across the river, the view is dominated by the fine house, Myddleton Lodge, on the brow of the hill. At the clubhouse **A** turn left onto the footpath that runs diagonally across the field to a kissing gate. To the left a row of rather dourly respectable villas spreads out along the main road. Follow the line of the fence and thorn hedge through a series of gates. After a short walk beside a stream, the path rejoins the river.

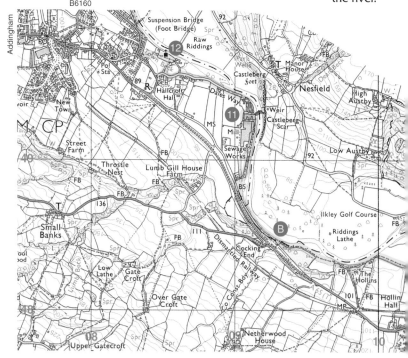

Cross a small footbridge and take the narrow riverside path, a mass of stones and gnarled tree roots. A slight rise affords an attractive view of the broad sweep of the river and the golf course opposite. Back at river level, boulders provide a convenient perch for the dippers, which will be constant companions throughout the riverside walk, as will the black-headed gull. Birdsong from the woods to the left competes with the roar of water over a series of small rapids. The path now joins the old Ilkley to Addingham road **B** with the busy new main road over to the left. The base of an old cast-iron gas lamp, with the gas pipe still poking up through the middle, serves as a reminder of a bygone age. Just before the houses, turn right down Old Lane to Smithy Greaves and Holme Ings, a housing development based on an old mill village originally known as Low Mills **11**. This is soon followed by High Mill, built in the 1780s for spinning cotton, using machinery powered by a water wheel. In the 1820s it was converted into a woollen mill, and by the 1860s silk was being spun here.

Leave the village by a gravel drive to join a waterside metalled road. The path follows a little backwater to the ornamental gardens of the Old Rectory. These are home to a collection of colourful ducks. Mandarin and Muscovy waddle around the more common mallards, while distant screeches announce the presence of peacocks. At the end of the stone wall, turn right to take the footpath down the steps towards the church. This is an attractive area, with the path heading away across the green to the cottages. It is worthwhile pausing to visit the church **12**, which has a painted gallery dating from 1757, under which is the base of a ninth-century cross, with two rather worn human figures.

From the church head across the green, cross the stone bridge to North Street and turn right. Do not cross the river – follow the road round to the left and then to the right, down cobbled streets, to join the riverside path. The route passes

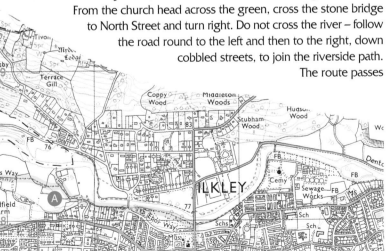

the High Mill complex **13** and an old open store with a roof supported on stone pillars. A large weir is the main feature on the river. The path now leads into a caravan park, but almost immediately turns right to follow a narrow footpath between the park and the riverbank. A wooden stile marks the end of this constricted area and the walk continues over open fields that run down to the water's edge. The river itself is wide and deep, a popular congregating area for mallard and moorhen. The path now runs through typical, lush meadowland – fields packed with dandelions, daisies and buttercups and divided off from the pasture by neat stone walls. A short climb up by an old barn provides a chance to enjoy the wider view. The path soon comes down to river-level again and leads to a prominent ladder stile, beyond which is a large wind-powered generator. The bird-life here establishes the pattern for the whole walk up Wharfedale: dippers and wagtails hop around the rocks while swifts and swallows make low-level raids, skimming the water for insects. The route now leads uphill to join the road **C**.

Dog's mercury and bluebells carpet the floor around the silver birch of a Wharfedale wood.

Until recently the official route ran along this busy and dangerous road and is still shown on many maps. But a new route was agreed in 1996 and this route should definitely be followed as it makes for a much pleasanter and less stressful walk. Turn left at the road then almost immediately right up the track leading to Lobwood House. Cross over the stone stile by the gate in the wall on the right to follow a footpath running parallel to the road. Ignore the stile on the right leading back towards the road, and continue on to cross the wall up ahead by a stone stile, followed by a footbridge over a stream. At the far end of the field, return to the road via the stile beside the gate. Cross straight over the busy road to take advantage of the footpath on the far side and continue along the road as far as a gate in the stone wall on the right. Cross the footbridge, rejoining the riverside path under the new road bridge, and take the stone steps up by the side of the old bridge. Cross over the road to take the path between the cricket field and the river, and rejoin the riverside path. The landscape begins to undergo subtle changes as rough moorland encroaches on the valley floor. The next objective, Bolton Priory, soon comes into view.

Bolton Priory: the roofed nave of what is now the parish church can be seen behind the magnificent ruined arch.

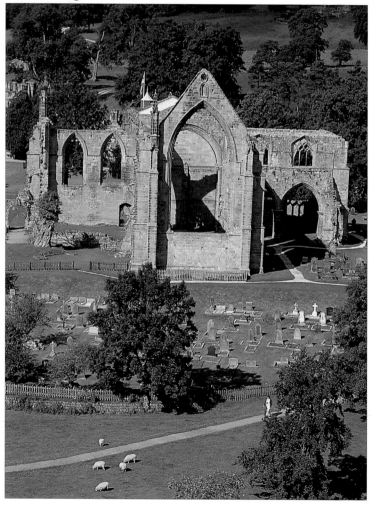

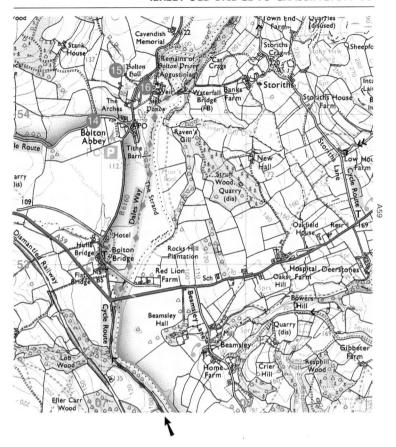

The local village, confusingly known as Bolton Abbey **14**, is over to the left, but the main focus of interest is down here by the river. First come the indentations (all that remain of the old Priory fish ponds), then Bolton Hall **15**, a very appealing Dales house of some grandeur. Beyond that is the Priory itself **16**, founded by the Augustinians in the middle of the twelfth century. The monks' ideals of poverty and silent meditation were modified over the years, and by the time Henry VIII brought all monastic life to an end, the Priory was a centre of immense wealth, with lands stretching far out from Wharfedale. Bolton was luckier than the majority of the great churches. The nave was preserved as an unusually magnificent parish church, but one cannot help looking at the ruined grandeur around it and mourning what was lost. The gatehouse was sold for the precisely recorded sum of £2,490 1s 1d to the Earl of Cumberland, who set about converting it to form part of Bolton Hall.

Looking out across Bolton Priory to the craggy hills at the edge of Wharfedale.

The route turns across the footbridge, close by a dramatic rock face that falls sheer to the water (those with a sense of adventure can use the stepping stones). Continue upstream on the opposite bank (a pleasant, easy stroll across grassland), following the line of trees at the bottom of the hill to cut across the looping bend of the river. Cross the stile, climb a little hillock and take the path through the woods. This is far more pleasant than the opposite bank which, in summer, is little better than a huge car park. The woodland contains holly and sycamore, but the dominant tree is the sessile oak, distinguished from its more familiar relation by its long leaves and stalkless acorns. The path has a crazy-paving effect of criss-crossed roots, and steadily climbs the bank to the rim before Duke of Yorking it back down again. Where the path emerges at the road, turn left and cross the stream either at the ford or the footbridge **D**. Immediately turn left to join the footpath by the river. Turn left again to cross the bridge over the river to the Cavendish Pavilion, which has refreshments on sale, then turn right to take the path through Strid Wood. Nature trails wander about here, but the Dales Way follows the line of the river. Once in the

A waterfall on Posforth Gill, which joins the Wharfe near The Strid.

woods you may get a whiff of sulphur from the sulphur well near Cowpert Gill. The river becomes ever more turbulent as it crashes its way through a jumble of rocks, hiding temporarily behind an island and then reappearing as a shallower stream, the colour of molasses. As the wooded gorge narrows so the scenery becomes more dramatic with boulders among the trees, and the river has its moment of high drama at The Strid **17**. Here the rocky walls close in, forcing the water to race and fall through a narrow opening. A small diversion is needed to see this, but it is well worth the effort. Over the years many foolish people have tried to leap The Strid; not all have survived to boast of it. From The Strid, a narrow path up through the rocks returns to the main track, which now runs at a high level, giving a good view of the rocky gorge and, as the woods thin out, of the hills and moorland up ahead. Cross the footbridge over a stream and then cross a stile to continue along the river's edge.

The route now arrives at a particularly grand stone footbridge **18**, with castellations in the best medieval manner. Why such grandeur? The answer is provided by a glance upstream. The bridge was in view from Barden Tower **19**, now an impressive ruin. The first tower was built in the eleventh century and restored in 1657 by the redoubtable Lady Anne Clifford. Future generations, however, showed no interest in the cold, draughty castle, but the priest's house and chapel provided by the tenth Lord Clifford in the fifteenth century are still there. Cross the footbridge and follow the path over the fields beside the river to Barden Bridge. This handsome structure is of uncertain age, but an inscription on the parapet declares it was 'repayred' in 1676. Do not cross the bridge but go straight on up the road. Where the road begins to go uphill turn off to continue on the path beside the river. This is an altogether gentler landscape of fields dotted with mature oak and sycamore, with a thin sprinkling of farms among the

Magnificent even in ruins: Barden Tower, which was home to Lady Anne Clifford in the seventeenth century.

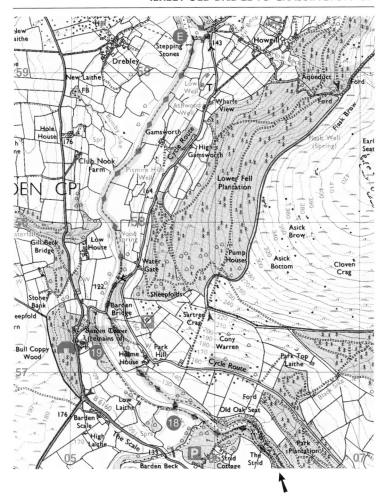

network of stone walls. The path stays close to the river's edge, while the upper slopes are soon covered in dense conifer plantations. Along this stretch, birds far outnumber humans: squadrons of swifts and martins patrol the river above an armada of mallards.

The grassy path gives way to a stony track leading uphill. By a set of stepping stones **E** the path leads temporarily away from the river towards a farm. Turn left at the road to cross the bridge over Fir Beck, which dashes down to the river in a series of small falls, then immediately turn left again through the gap in the stone wall, by the sign saying 'Footpath to Appletreewick and Burnsall'. The path cuts across the field to the woods by the river. Here is another of the Wharfe's little

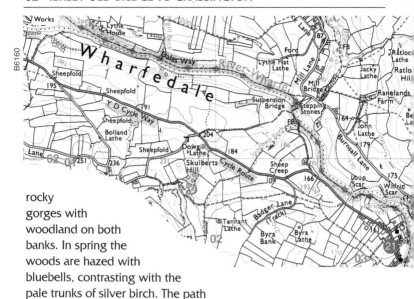

rocky
gorges with
woodland on both
banks. In spring the
woods are hazed with
bluebells, contrasting with the
pale trunks of silver birch. The path
returns to the water's edge, and the pleasant village of Appletreewick
20 can be seen stretching out on the ridge to the right, its main street
climbing from Low Hall at one end to High Hall at the other. The village, with its good grazing and its lead mines, was once a possession
of Bolton Priory. A charter of 1311 allowed for an annual Onion Fair to
be held – now remembered in the name of little Onion Lane. The village is only a short walk from the Dales Way, but the route itself
remains firmly fixed to the river.

As the Way continues up Wharfedale, changes begin to appear in
the land as the dark gritstone gives way to paler limestone. Kail Hill,
up to the right, is a pleasant, shapely green mound, but there were
once lead mines beneath its surface. Where the path divides by a
camp site, stay with the riverside path, signposted to Burnsall. Here
the river is in gentle mood, its banks sprinkled with marsh marigolds.
Where the way along the bank is barred by a stone wall **F**, turn right to
follow the path along the side of the wall towards the farm buildings,
and pass between the attractive traditional farmhouse and the equally
traditional barn with an exterior stone staircase. Where the track
divides, turn left over the first bridge and cross the stone stile in the
corner of the field to rejoin the river. Burnsall Bridge now comes into
view but, as the river turns away to the left, the path goes straight on,
heading for the gate at the end of the impressive causeway that leads
up to the bridge itself. The Way goes straight over the bridge and then
turns right to rejoin the riverside path. Burnsall itself, however, is not

to be overlooked. It has a special place in the affections of those who regard simply walking the Dales as altogether too tame, for it is the starting point of Britain's oldest fell race. Many of the houses have the small, mullioned windows of the seventeenth century, but the village itself is far older. There are Norse crosses of the ninth and tenth centuries in the churchyard **21**, while the church was built in the twelfth century, although largely rebuilt in the sixteenth. It still retains a magnificent medieval Adoration of the Magi – and do look out for the curious seventeenth-century turnstile at the lych gate. The primary school next door was founded in Tudor times as a grammar school, with the old village stocks nearby as a warning to badly behaved pupils.

Returning now to the bridge, take the stony path behind the church. Leaving the village, one enters one of the most dramatic parts of the walk. Here the river races along beneath tall limestone crags reminiscent of some of the famous Derbyshire dales. The walk slips briefly into a little wooded area of mainly sycamore and beech, then crosses the river on a suspension bridge. The bank on this side is lined with an impressive row of mature trees, with some particularly grand horse chestnuts. This is a very calm, peaceful area of smooth grassland, grazed by sheep, with the steep valley sides closing off the wider views. The only signs of busy activity come from the resident population of birds.

The artificial weir and natural waterfalls at Linton.

Where the river swings away to the left, head for the footbridge in the field **G**. Continue on towards the church now visible up ahead, and return to the riverside. Go through the gate onto the wide stony track, past the house that overhangs the water, to the road. Where the road bends sharply to the right, cross the stone stile and take the grassy track back once again to the river. The church on the opposite bank is, somewhat surprisingly, Grassington parish church, a survivor from the days when the parishes of Grassington and Linton were combined. A feature of the river is the so-called Linton Falls, in fact two artificial weirs **22**, built to provide water power for the local woollen mill. This was established in 1790 and almost survived to reach its bicentenary; now all that remains are the mill cottages and the sluices to control the water. Between the two weirs turn away from the river to follow a path to the right of the stone wall, passing the foot of the hillside. Carry on past the row of houses to the bridge and turn right for the centre of Grassington.

3 GRASSINGTON TO HUBBERHOLME

via Kettlewell   *12 miles (19 km)*

One of the delights of the Dales Way is the variety of the landscape. This stage is a complete contrast to the last, exchanging airy limestone upland for shady river valley. But before that stage is reached, there is Grassington itself to explore. Take the footpath up the hill to the cross-roads, and go straight on up the main street, which opens out into a cobbled square surrounded by fine old stone buildings, one of which now houses the Upper Wharfedale Museum **23**. From this centre a complex of little lanes and alleys lead away invitingly – and rarely disappoint. One curiosity at the top of Garrs Lane is Theatre Cottage, originally a barn but once indeed converted into a theatre where Edmund Kean, one of the most famous actors of the Victorian age, came to astound local audiences. Those sticking resolutely to the line of the Dales Way should go straight up the High Street, passing a little cobbled lane on the left, where one of the old cottages is carved with a wedding date, *LN and HW 1751*. At the town hall **A**, once the local mechanics' institute, turn left down Chapel Street. The Grassington circular walk also starts here (see p. 78).

Grassington is a village of reassuring solidity, its stone houses clustering together in tight knots, defying anything the weather might bring. At the end of the lane, go into the farmyard and follow the route marked by yellow arrows to emerge on the fell side. The path immediately divides and the Way follows the high-level route to the right, signposted 'Footpath to Conistone'. Already the walk has gained a considerable height and there are immense, wide views out over Wharfedale. This is an area of ancient settlement and, down to the left, regular humps and hollows represent the tumbled walls and foundations of medieval village houses **24**, surrounded by an extraordinary pattern of tiny fields of all shapes and sizes. Take the right hand of two gates and head across the field to the squeeze stile. There can be no question now that the walk has reached the heart of the limestone country. Gone is the soft roundedness of the valley; the landscape has become altogether more angular. Small rocky outcrops burst through the tops of hills and, at the valley's edge, the lip is laid out in a natural limestone pavement.

The route now passes through a second, even more distinct, medieval village **25**. On either side are the neat squares and oblongs of former houses and barns, while large clumps of nettles indicate the likely site of old rubbish tips. Go through a stile, with a limestone pavement on the left, and join the obvious green track, heading slightly to the right. There is something of a multiplicity of tracks in this area, but the main route runs parallel to a stone wall on the right. A tremendous view of typical limestone upland now presents itself – sweeping hills, carved up by walls, with flat stone beds cut into neat blocks by the frost. Where the walls meet **B**, look for a big wooden ladder stile on the right-hand side. The path now heads to the right of the limestone outcrop. There is a clear line to follow, marked by obvi-

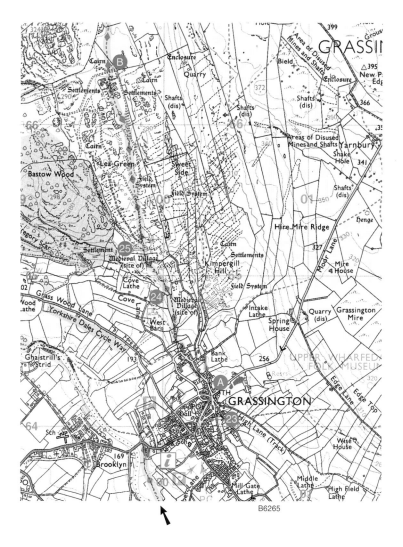

B6265

The old stone houses and cobbled streets combine to make picturesque Grassingto

...e of the most popular tourist spots in the Dales.

ous stiles, towards the left-hand side of the limestone outcrop on the horizon. Within the little hollow is a lime kiln, crudely constructed out of big, unshaped boulders. Lime was once an important fertiliser, and it was not unknown for an individual farmer to run his own kiln. The kiln itself was loaded with alternate layers of coal and broken stone and the lime raked out at the bottom.

The way divides, one path heading downhill to Conistone, but the main route goes straight ahead **C** towards the bottom of the rocky scar on the right. It then crosses a steep-sided rocky gully, a spectacular cleft in the hillside, to carry straight on below the edge of the escarpment. Up ahead is a rocky pinnacle with a cairn on top, known as Conistone Pie. This is literally one of the high points of the walk, offering some of the best views of the entire journey. Just across the river are the well-known, fiercely overhanging rock faces of Kilnsey Crag.

Here, too, one can see the classic pattern of Dales farming spread out like a text-book diagram. The valley bottom is a complex of small fields, demarcating pasture that will provide winter feed, while the long walls straggle up

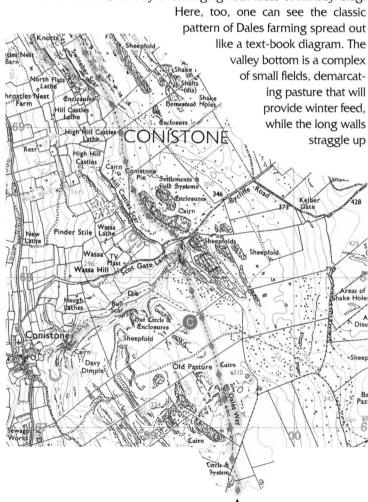

A fine example of a limestone pavement alongside the Dales Way on the escarpment above Grassington.

The ancient pattern of small irregular fields seen from Conistone Pie. In the distance, Old Cote Moor rises over the junction of Littondale and Wharfedale.

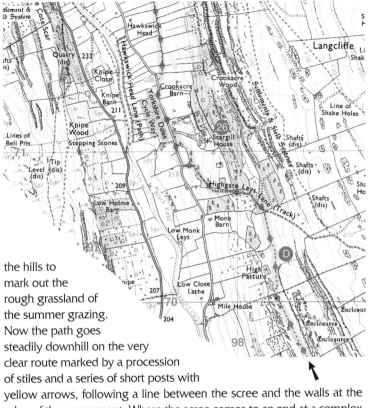

the hills to
mark out the
rough grassland of
the summer grazing.
Now the path goes
steadily downhill on the very
clear route marked by a procession
of stiles and a series of short posts with
yellow arrows, following a line between the scree and the walls at the
edge of the escarpment. Where the scree comes to an end at a complex
of walls **D**, head towards the conifers and the short stone wall to the left.
Cross the stile to take the broad track through the woods, which curls
away to go steadily downhill. Now that the windswept uplands have
been left behind, the sheltered slopes offer a home to delicate plants
such as cowslips. The upland excursion is over.

Returning to the valley floor can bring its own rewards: the author
came upon a weasel enjoying a sunbathe on top of a wall. Buildings
return, notably Scargill House **26**, now a religious centre with a new
church, and what a pleasure it is to see a building that is at once clearly
modern yet which fits so well into this traditional landscape. The roof
sweeps steeply down in a plunging curve that almost overwhelms the
walls with their narrow openings. At the roadway, turn right to follow
the lane through a complex of narrow fields. Where the road swings
round to the left, turn right through a wooden gate signposted
'Footpath to Kettlewell', then almost immediately left through a second
gate. The path follows an obvious line, keeping to the wall but frequently

The village of Kettlewell sitting in a snug hollow. Here the Dales Way comes down from the hill to rejoin the river valley.

hopping from one side to the other, with yellow dots used as way-markers. When you reach a green lane at the edge of Kettlewell **E** do not cross the stile, but turn left down the lane and then right onto the farm track by the large horse-chestnut trees to pass the edge of the churchyard. The church itself **27** is mainly Victorian, but has turned its back on glum Gothic in favour of a pleasing light airiness, enhanced by stained glass from the William Morris studios. At the road turn left into the village centre. Kettlewell is a quiet, unassuming place, with a stream trickling at the roadside, a number of stone cottages and no less than three pubs, reflecting its former importance as a river crossing on the old Wharfedale coach road. Cross the bridge over a tributary stream to the main road, signposted to Burnsall, then cross another bridge, turning right through a wooden gate and immediately right again to join the riverside path.

Now the walk has much more of the character of the previous section, except that the river has shrunk a great deal since it was last encountered. On the Grassington-to-Kettlewell walk, however, one looked down from the wide spaces to view the intricate field pattern of the valley. Here the fields are experienced as a seemingly endless succession of gates and stiles, and the hills provide the grand views beyond. The path at first stays close to the river's edge, then turns slightly away to pass through a small copse before joining a farm track. The route, crossed by a number of springs, cuts across a very regular pattern of fields, divided by walls set at right angles to the river. The landscape pattern is now that of a glaciated valley, with flat bottom and smooth, rounded sides. Where the drystone walls that have bounded the lane come to an end, continue across the fields through the obvious wall gaps. Beyond two ladder stiles, the path deserts the farm track, turning right towards the corner of the stone walls, then follows the wall down to the river **F**. It is all very pleasant, easy walking; the path remains more or less straight while the river goes into convulsions, turning right back on itself in an extravagant hairpin bend. A pattern is established with the Way alternating between riverbank paths and other paths that avoid the marshy ground created round the meanders.

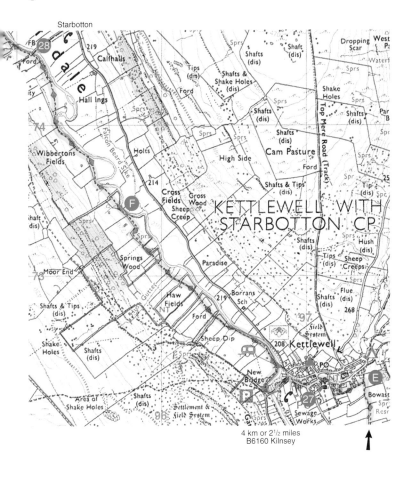

4 km or 2¹/₂ miles
B6160 Kilnsey

Villages and settlements congregate on the opposite bank. An iron footbridge **28** provides access to Starbotton, offering an attractive temporary detour for those with time to spare. The village has an air of comfortable antiquity, and offers an extra inducement in the Fox and Hounds pub. Meanwhile the riverside route continues on its way past the remnants of an old packhorse route leading off on the left over the hills to Arncliffe. The country seems for a while to be tamed after the craggy landscape around Kettlewell: the limestone is little more than a pale line stretched across the hillside opposite, while over to the left the slopes are clad in dense woodland. The route is equally gentle, an undemanding stroll across grassland. Where the river goes off on one of its longer excursions, continue straight on along the path by the stone wall. The damp meadows to the right are bright with marsh marigolds and the occasional marsh orchid, while the cry of the lapwing, which will become ever more common as the walk heads off towards the moor, echoes over the valley. Listening to the birds' distinctive cries, it is easy to see why locals prefer the alternative name of 'peewit'.

The path now becomes a farm track, running between stone walls. A footbridge crosses Step Gill, which can be anything from a dry bed of stones to a respectable torrent, depending on the weather. The hillside to the left is notable for a splendid array of tall, mature trees, showing a wonderful mixture of colours from the pale greens of the birch to the deep hues of the conifers. As the path draws close to the wood, a copper beech supplies a sudden, startling burst of colour. Turn off to the right and return to the wandering river, following this all the way to Buckden Bridge. This village's main claims to fame are its very attractive pub, and the home-made nettle beer on sale at the shop. Turn left at the bridge **29** then immediately right, taking the path through the trees to the river. This is once again a genuine riverside walk. Giant boulders provide flood protection, while rocks in the stream give a perch to one of the more colourful of the wagtail family, the yellow wagtail.

Where the riverbank is closed off by wall and fence **G**, turn left to follow the wall down to the road, and then turn right. The walk now leads on to Hubberholme and the beginning of Langstrothdale.

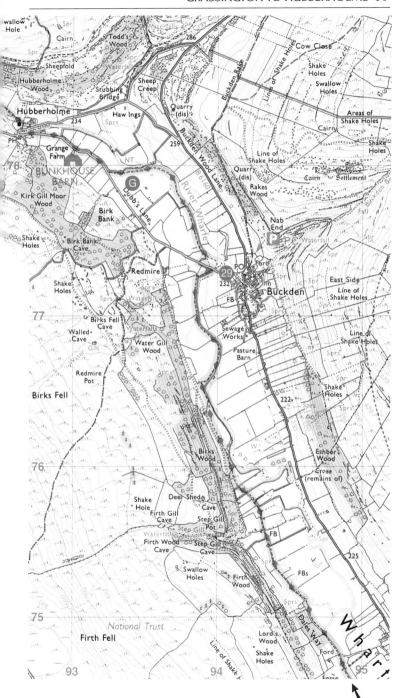

CIRCULAR WALK FROM GRASSINGTON

5 miles (8 km)

The walk begins at Grassington Town Hall **A**. Continue straight on up the hill on the road marked 'No Through Road'. This climbs steeply between stone walls and passes a former hill farm, now converted for furniture making, with a small quarry opposite. Just beyond a small farmhouse and barn on the right, and before the hill begins to steepen, turn right to cross a stone stile **B** on a path signposted 'Hebden Bridleway'. Head for the tall smelt mill chimney on the horizon. To the right of the path a very regular ring of stones can be seen **30**, a henge monument dating back to the Neolithic or New Stone Age.

Cross the fields, heading first for a small gated stile in the wall, and then continue on through a gap in the next wall to another stile. Soon one enters a landscape entirely dominated by the scars and spoil heaps of lead mining. The path becomes a broad track, around which are deep hollows surrounded by grassed-over rings of spoil that mark the position of old bell pits. At the wide level track **C** turn right. Over to the left a hump in the ground leads straight up the hill; this is the flue from the smelt mill, and ends at the tall chimney on the horizon. To the right is a small reservoir that in the eighteenth century provided water to power pumps and ore-crushing machinery. The main centre of activity, just to the right of the track, was centred on the 360-ft-deep Union shaft **31**, now protected by a metal grille.

The track continues on past a wooden gate **D**, then turns left to zigzag down to the top of Hebden Beck. Turn right here, keeping the stream on the left. A suspended fence acts as a barrier for stock, but floats on its hinges when the stream is in flood. Just before a ruined building, cross over to the opposite side at a ford. Shortly afterwards, a drainage adit can be seen on the left, used for removing water from the mineworkings. It is followed by an extensive area of arched adits leading deep into the hillside, together with shafts, wheel pits, ruined buildings and spoil heaps.

At Hole Bottom **E** cross the bridge over the stream and carry on down to the road that leads steeply downhill along the side of the gill. The road arrives at the delightful village of Hebden **32**. Go down to the junction and turn right at the main road, passing the Clarendon

Hotel. Take the second of two footpaths **F**, signposted 'Grassington via High Lane'. Once across the stone stile, head for a small gate next to a metal gate. Make for the far right-hand corner of the field and cut across a narrow strip of woodland to emerge by the semi-derelict buildings of an old hospital. The way in front of the buildings is marked by wooden posts. Head for the far corner, cross the driveway and take the path by the copse. Continue across the field, keeping the wall to the left. Cross the stony track by two stone stiles, following the farm track round to a gateway with a stone stile alongside. At this point the farm track turns left towards a barn, but the footpath continues straight on over a series of stiles. Eventually it becomes a track running between stone walls towards Grassington. At the roadway turn right to return to the start.

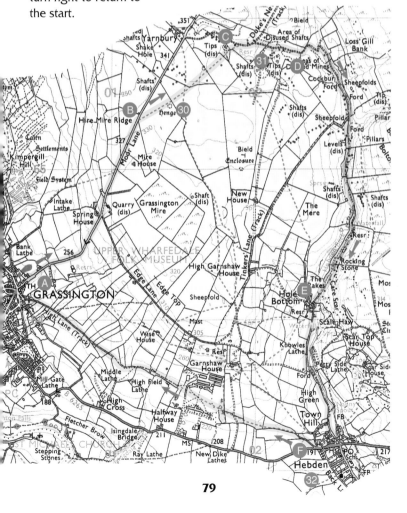

A typical Dales waterfall over limestone ledges, Buckden Beck.

4 HUBBERHOLME TO DENT HEAD VIADUCT

via Yockenthwaite and Cam Houses   *14 miles (22.5 km)*

This is the most demanding section of the walk, offering yet more land-scape variations and new grandeurs as one crosses the watershed on the high moor. The valley of the Wharfe will be left behind for the delights of Dentdale, but first there is Hubberholme itself to enjoy. The George Inn is everything a country pub should be – even if it was origi-nally built as a vicarage. Outside it is plain and sturdy, inside it has stone-flagged floors and simple furniture. Each year at the inn, the rights to one of the local fields are auctioned off: a candle is lit and the bids begin. The last bid to be made before the candle dies secures the rights.

The walk now crosses the picturesque bridge to reach the church **33**. This is perhaps the loveliest of all Dales churches, notable for its elaborate rood loft and screen. The modern pews are by Robert Thompson and each carries his distinctive mark, a tiny carved mouse. The circular walk that starts here brings its own pleasures (see p. 94).

To continue on the Dales Way, take the footpath that goes round the church wall to follow the river upstream. Although this is still the Wharfe, it is easy to see why this valley has a different name, Langstrothdale. Where the river in Wharfedale ran generally from north to south down a wide valley, here it runs from west to east, carving a narrower valley, tightly closed in by high hills. At first the path struggles through a thorn thicket, but it soon opens out to a more comfortable grassy track. Over to the left is moorland of grass and bracken, while on this side of the river the sheltered south-facing slope is covered with trees. Crossing a stile **A**, turn left towards the riverbank and follow the line of the riverside wall. A footbridge takes the path across a stream that in wet weather cascades over a series of ledges, but in a dry spell can be reduced to a trickle. This is true of the main stream as well, with its series of falls created by a staircase of flat, rocky ledges. The route is the obvious riverside path through a multitude of walls crossed by stiles and gates, or simply with gaps in the stonework.

The view from Buckden Pike, looking down Langstrothdale towards the little village

f Hubberholme. In the distance is the dark bulk of Oughtershaw Moor.

Yockenthwaite **B** is not so much a place as a cluster of farmhouses and barns. Head towards the farm buildings and, just before the iron gate, turn right to cross a stone stile, then immediately left to walk through the wooden gate to pass above the farm. This is a most attractive hamlet in an idyllic setting. The Wharfe rushes under a high-arched stone bridge, and the elegant houses manage to seem at home even in such a remote valley. The walk passes a house with a very grand entrance and a pedimented front door, and leads up through the farm buildings to merge into a broad track above the river. The road on the opposite side by the grassy bank and rocky ledges makes this a popular picnic site, while the flat rock bed makes the river ideal for children to paddle in. A reminder of the working life of the dale appears in the shape of a small lime kiln. The rounded hills to either side are now dotted with stunted trees and patched with bracken. An archaeological curiosity is a small stone circle **34**, roughly six metres across, with three outlying stones that suggest there may once have been a second ring. Its date and purpose are equally obscure.

At a stone stile leading to a field **C**, the path turns away from the river to head for an obvious gap in the stone wall to the right of a barn and, beyond that, to a ladder stile. Once across the stile, turn right to follow the line of the wall across the field. Head downhill to cross the footbridge over Deepdale Gill, which unlike many in the area has a permanent flow of water. Take the path in front of the farm and turn left onto the farm track. Deepdale is a small hamlet, like Yockenthwaite, and again boasts some handsome houses. One up the hill has an impressive Gothic entrance and a big, bold external chimney. Cross over the road bridge and continue on the opposite bank of the river. The track leads past a farm which enjoys a delightful situation, with a small waterfall right outside the front door. As the path goes ever higher up the dale,

a number of springs and streams trickling off the moor make the way a little muddy in places. The river and the streams have continued to shape the stones and boulders into satisfyingly rich, curved shapes: it is not too difficult to see where Yorkshire sculptors Barbara Hepworth and Henry Moore received their inspiration. Beyond a ladder stile by a complex of rocks and little falls, the path comes out into more open country, grassland taking over from the stony track. As the hillside begins to close in on the left, keep to the rocky riverbank and head for the footbridge **D**. Cross the bridge and follow the lane round to the road, turn right across the bridge and turn left at the road junction, in the direction signposted to Hawes.

Langstrothdale is now left behind and the hillsides are entirely blanketed with conifers, while the Way itself heads off towards open moorland. The road climbs steeply up one side of a deep gorge with the infant River Wharfe at the bottom. At the roadside there is a small drinking trough, fed by a stream emerging from a cleft in the rock. This is a lumpy, craggy landscape with patches of woodland developing wherever there is enough shelter for trees to grow. Oughtershaw Hall is a suitably tough-looking building in this environment and shows the typical features of the area: stone mullioned windows with dripstones above and a stone slate roof. It looks as if it has been here for centuries, but is in fact Victorian. The river, now scarcely more than a stream, comes into sight again. In this remarkably stony landscape, plant life has to survive as best it can: one tenacious tree has knotted its roots around the boulders, which are like stones held in a giant's hand.

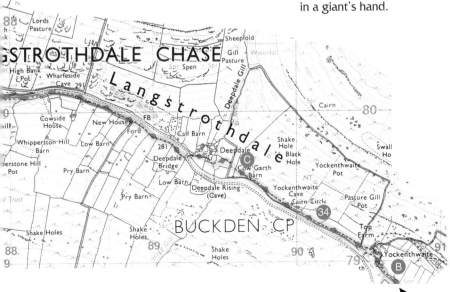

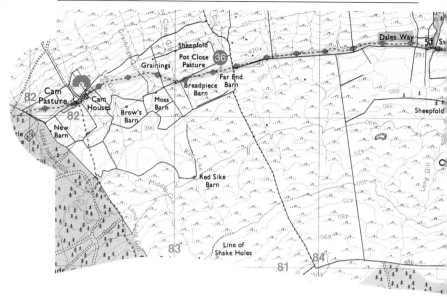

The road goes downhill to Oughtershaw
bunkhouse and an extraordinary little building
of highly polished marble **35**, originally built as a school to a design by
John Ruskin. Immediately past Hazelbank Farm and just before the
large 'Celtic' cross (actually erected for Victoria's jubilee), turn left **E**
onto the broad stony track that marks the start of a walk across the
moor and across the watershed.

The river is now reduced to a beck, yet seems if anything to support an even larger, busier bird population than the lower river. It is a
pleasant place to pause now that the road is left behind. Grey and yellow wagtails, martins, swallows and dippers can be seen, while the
peewits, even if they are not necessarily in view, are rarely out of
earshot. The track and stream separate, and the former runs past the
lonely farmstead of Nethergill. This is a hard area for farmers to earn
a living. The rich, nourishing grass of the lower Dales has now given
way to the coarse, spiky clumps of the fells, and the poorer grazing
means that farms have to be more widely scattered. The Way goes on
across an increasingly bare, open landscape with little but the occasional song of the skylark for company. A mile or so up the track,
Nethergill's nearest neighbour, Swarthgill, appears – the ideal place
to live for those who are content with their own company. Here the
broad track comes to an end, and the moorland path begins. Go past
the house to the iron gate in the wall and follow the path, keeping the
wall on the left.

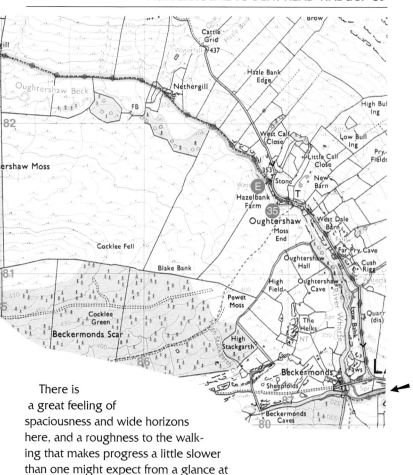

There is a great feeling of spaciousness and wide horizons here, and a roughness to the walking that makes progress a little slower than one might expect from a glance at the map, which only hints at the ups and downs. Little detours are necessary to cross the streams, and there are patches of boggy peat to be avoided or endured. Crossing a short ladder stile, head towards the field barns. This part of the walk is now very close to the watershed **36**. Streams no longer head east to join a system that will eventually end at the North Sea, but are now on their way to the Irish Sea. Aim for the larger of the two barns, cross the stile in front of the barn, then turn right to cross the ladder stile and head diagonally up towards the Cam Houses farm. Go through the farmyard, past a wooden barn, turn left onto the roadway, go through an iron gate in front of the stone barns, through a second iron gate and over a stile. Go down a short lane between walls, then head diagonally towards the uphill end of the conifer plantation. As you get nearer the woods,

Ingleborough with its distinctive stepped appearance dominates the landscape to the south of Dentdale.

head for the white footpath sign. Cross the stile and take the invariably muddy path up the side of the woods. At the end of the wood, go straight across the broad track onto the narrow footpath, heading diagonally uphill. Follow the line of the fence to cross a stile, then continue on the diagonal to a post on the horizon.

This post marks the point where the Dales Way and the Pennine Way briefly join. Turn left onto the broad track. This is Cam High Road **37**, built by the Romans in the first century AD as part of a military network to keep the Brigantes in check. In later years it was used as a drove road, as a packhorse route by wool merchants and later as a general highway. More recently it has become a playground for four-wheel-drive vehicles, which have contrived to do more damage in the last ten years than the rest of the users in almost two thousand. However worn the ancient way may have become, nothing can detract from the magnificence of the view, which on a good day takes in all Three Peaks, Whernside, Pen-y-ghent and Ingleborough, while leaving the massive Dent Head Viaduct looking like something out of a toy train set. Closer at hand in the summer months, cheerful meadow pipits keep the walker company. The route divides here **F**, the Pennine Way heading off to the left and the Dales Way carrying straight on. Up ahead, the moorland rolls forward in a series of rounded humps towards the

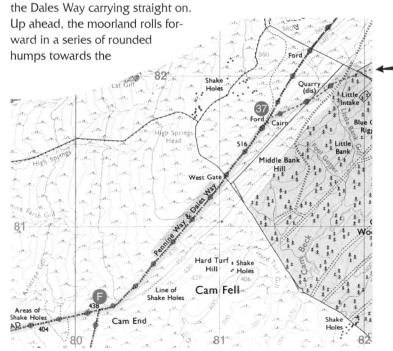

lusher green of the valley. The walk now passes a line of grouse butts, which can be quite interesting between 12 August and 10 December
. At the bottom of the hill, a footbridge crosses Gayle Beck and the track leads up to the road. It is worthwhile making a small detour to the left to see a cave which disappears into the hillside, its end lost in the inky dark. At the road turn left, passing an old milestone from the days of the turnpike trust, announcing to travellers that they are on the Lancaster to Richmond Road. This is Gearstones **38**, where there was once an inn that was one of the most important stopping places on the old drove road between Scotland and England. At this point turn right onto the surfaced track. There are hints here of changes in the landscape. The Dent Fault is an area where older rocks, typical of those found in the Lake District, have pushed their way through the limestone, and they first appear in this pathway as slate-green fragments. At Winshaw House, do not cross over the stile on the right, but go round in front of the house and take the path that climbs up a steep little hill beside the wall **G**. This is typical, peaty heather moorland, where one is quite likely to surprise a grouse that will set off on a low-level flight with a noisy whirr of wings and a hoarse cry. Where the wall turns to the right, just beyond the whitewashed farm, carry straight on. At the wooden signpost **H**, continue along the broad grassy track, which can make a pleasant change from squelchy peat. The path appears to peter out by a small stream with multiple crossing points, but is easily picked up again on the far side, heading in the same direction. It continues as a ledge on the side of the hill, crosses straight over a farm track between fences, then over a small footbridge. Although the path keeps to an obvious route there are numerous small diversions to avoid boggy areas. Once again, this has to be allowed for in estimating walking times. At the roadway turn left.

Whether the road is regarded as a welcome relief or an unfortunate interruption will very much depend on the weather, but it is certainly easy walking through attractive scenery, going steadily downhill to Dent Head Viaduct **39**. Seen close to, this is even more impressive than from a distance. Built out of massive stones it is also a tribute to the masons' art, for it is set on the skew with the arch stones laid out in diagonals. For the engineers and navvies who built it more than a century ago, it was just another obstacle to be overcome in a grim and hostile land; to the walkers who now come this way it forms a triumphant arch of welcome into Dentdale. And to put it in perspective one has only to compare it with the tiny packhorse bridge, all but forgotten beneath its hundred-foot-high arches, which carried the traffic of the area before the railway arrived.

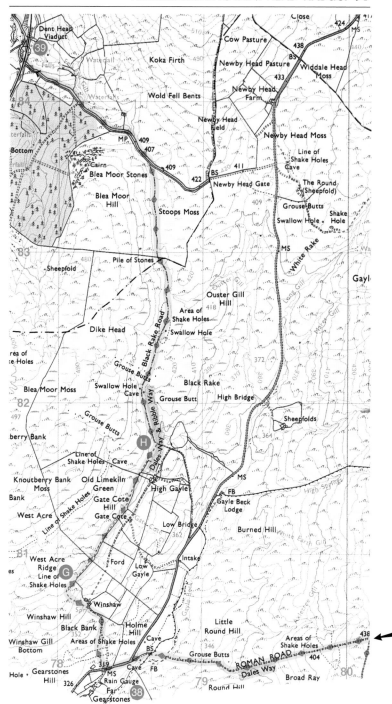

The view down Dentdale, seen from above the railway line.

CIRCULAR WALK FROM HUBBERHOLME

4 ½ miles (7.5 km)

Starting at Hubberholme church **A** take the stony track uphill sign-posted to Scar House. As the road begins to zigzag to cope with the steeper slope, one can see over to the left how naturally positioned boulders have been incorporated into the stone wall. The track emerges by a sturdy farmhouse, on which an inscription proclaims a wedding in 1698. Follow the track on round the house, turning sharp right **B** through a complex of low limestone crags to join the path above the woods. As the walk continues, the limestone underfoot widens to form a pavement weathered into blocks, in between which a solitary tree has found a home. Beyond a gap in the wall, the walker is presented with a flat grass terrace. There are low crags to the side and the hill to the left is topped by a small cairn **40**. The view extends right down the hollowed-out glacial scoop of Wharfedale. A more extensive limestone pavement appears, fractured into widely dispersed blocks, while a footbridge **C** crosses a narrow gully, whose stream makes a dramatic sight when in spate.

Turn right across the bridge. The track veers away from the gully, heading slightly uphill. Pass in front of the barn, go through the iron gate and continue on a grassy track across the meadows. The change of direction provides a view of the opposite hillside, eroded into terraces. The footpath passes behind a farmhouse and barns; where the way divides, keep to the left. Cross over a small stream and go through the farmyard with its pavement of natural stone, following the track down to the road by the White Lion Inn **D**. Cross the road and go over the stream on the stepping stones; a little waterfall and a packhorse bridge are over to the left. Follow the path by the wall, signposted 'Footpath to Cray Bridge and Buckden'. It swings round to the left before climbing to a gate in the wall. At the gateway turn right on the path signposted to Buckden. At the metal gate by the finger-post, continue along the stone wall. The path now becomes very rocky as it heads down towards Buckden. To one side trees cling tenaciously to the steep slope, while to the other rocks have shattered to create rough scree. Eventually the path emerges at the car park in Buckden **E**.

Turn left onto the road and right at the triangular green. The route passes a fine manor house **41** with a datestone of 1691 and a flagstone courtyard. Cross over Buckden Bridge and carry on down the lane. The small cairn passed earlier on the walk can now be seen on the right, marking the highest point visible from the valley floor. The Dales Way comes in here and the road is followed back to Hubberholme.

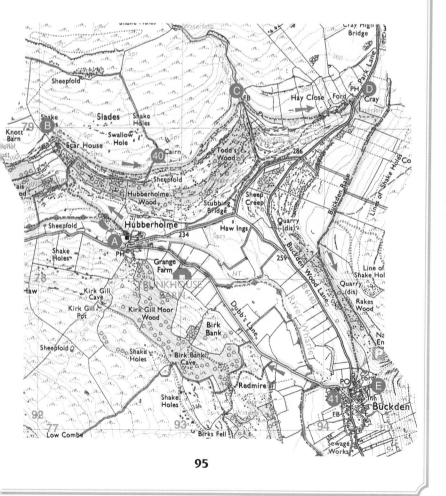

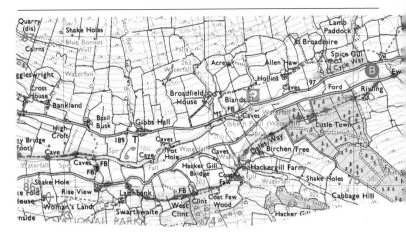

5 DENT HEAD TO MILLTHROP

via Dent   *11 ½ miles (18.5 km)*

After the high-level walk across the moors, this next stage comes as a complete contrast, both in terms of scenery and energy expended. It continues along the road for two and a half miles (4 km) and some walkers prefer to look for alternative, albeit longer, routes through the hills. This description, however, will stay with the official Dales Way.

The road runs beside a deep gill, where the stream races down over boulders. Eventually it comes down to the valley floor of Dentdale, keeping the busy stream as a constant companion. A neat little stone bridge leads to an attractive whitewashed house, which is now the Youth Hostel, and just beyond that the water tumbles over one of the larger limestone ledges, a grand enough fall to be blessed with a name, Scow Force **42**. A small lime kiln can be seen near the road, quite likely used by just one or possibly two farmers to produce lime for their own land. Stone House, which stands by Artengill Beck, owes its name to its former use as a Victorian 'marble' works, using the local black marble, a form of limestone with a high carbon content. The road crosses the infant River Dee on an attractive bridge, elegantly built with a corbelled corner to take the curve as it turns across the water. The cross-over makes little difference to the walk as it continues beside the river to The Sportsman's Arms, a pleasant whitewashed inn in an equally pleasant setting. Here the river runs down over a series of ledges and, through the clear water, the bed can be seen to be made up of large, flat slabs. The road again crosses the river and heads towards Dent Station, the

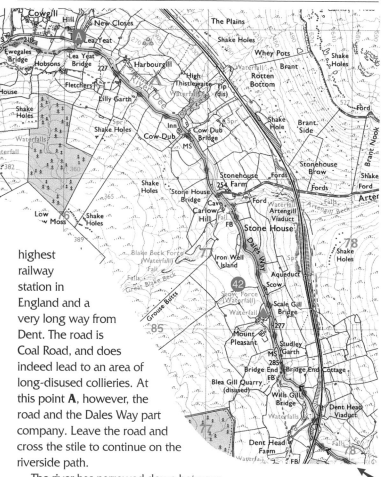

highest
railway
station in
England and a
very long way from
Dent. The road is
Coal Road, and does
indeed lead to an area of
long-disused collieries. At
this point **A**, however, the
road and the Dales Way part
company. Leave the road and
cross the stile to continue on the
riverside path.

The river has narrowed down between
rocky banks, but the footpath soon opens out to riverside meadows.
After this brief saunter through the fields to Ewegales Bridge, join the
narrow road that leads up to the farm and turn left through a gate by a
sign to Laithbank **B**. Head towards the farm buildings, but turn off
before reaching them, towards the remnants of a stone wall. Cross a little bridge over the beck, then cross the stile and take the path through
the typically dead, dense and dark conifer plantation. Leave the wood
by a couple of stiles, and cross the clearing, heading for the stile at the
next patch of woodland. Once clear of the woods, the pattern of
Dentdale becomes apparent. The hills rise steeply on either side. The
path runs along the lower edge of Whernside, which rises to a summit
of 2,414 ft (736 m); opposite is Aye Gill Pike at a more modest 1,824 ft

Dent Station on the Settle and Carlisle Railway, one of the most dramatic rail route

Britain.

Small farms, each with its patchwork of fields, scattered along the valley bottom in Dentdale.

(556 m). In between is the fertile valley floor with farms dotted at regular intervals, each with its complex of small uneven fields, following boundaries probably first laid down by the early Norse settlers. Above them, the stone walls run straight and true to the summit.

Leaving the plantation by the wooden stile, carry on to a squeeze stile and follow the line of the wall, through a second squeeze stile which genuinely earns its name – there is just about space enough to get a leg through. Cross another stone stile to take the broad farm track, which provides a fine view out over the whole dale. This part of the route is waymarked with yellow dots – be careful not to be misled by patches of lichen. Turn off the track to head for a stile by a solitary tree. The Way then contours the hill towards the next gate and a neat little farmhouse. Turn left **C** onto another track and follow it round to the right past the farm. Take the ladder stile to the right and head diagonally across the next field towards another ladder stile. Once over the stile, follow the wall round to the right. This is a rugged hillside, with a line of crags over to the left. Head for the whitewashed house and take the path round the back of the buildings. Cross the small footbridge and head towards the right-hand side of a section of isolated wall, then go through the gap in the wall opposite. Follow the broad track in front of the farm but, where the track bends round by the wall, continue straight on through the stone stile. Cross the beck on a footbridge and take the path that runs round the shoulder of the hill in front of a barn, turning left through the iron gate to take the stony track down to the road **D**.

Turn left at the road, bordered by a hedge above a bank full of aromatic wild garlic. Turn right through an iron gate and head down towards the river. Go straight across the field and down the steps to a footbridge, then turn left to follow the stream. Cut across the next field to a second bridge and cross over to turn left along the riverbank. The river in this area is somewhat curious: in dry weather it is likely to do temporary disappearing acts, leaving nothing but a bed of boulders – before reappearing in full flow. Grey-green slates are easily seen in the riverbed, a colourful prelude to the Lakeland rocks that lie ahead. Cross the river at the small footbridge known as the Tommy Bridge,

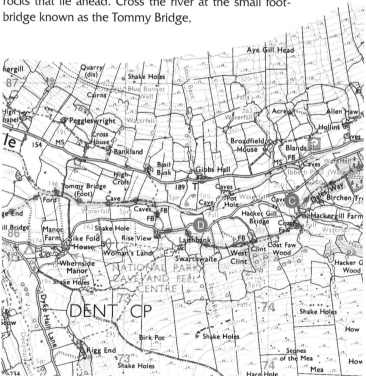

and turn right along the wall, past a farm track that leads down to a cattle ford. Cross the stone stile to the left of the iron gate and follow the path uphill beside the stone wall. The way across the field is marked by a post with a yellow arrow. Once over the brow of the hill, head for the large copper beech at the end of the wall and cross the ladder stile onto the road. Take the road across the bridge over the small stream, then turn immediately right again by the sign indicating the public footpath to Church Bridge.

Follow the path beside the turbulent little stream, and turn left at the junction with the river, heading along the bank, which has been built up with boulders as flood protection. The path is then diverted away from the river **E**. Cross a footbridge over a stream and turn right to the road bridge. The Dales Way now goes straight on along the riverbank, but it would be almost criminal to miss the village of Dent itself, just a stroll away to the left. It is included in the circular walk that starts here (see p. 108).

The village of Dent with its rough cobbled streets and whitewashed stone houses represents, for many people, the ideal Dales village.

The rough-hewn granite memorial to Adam Sedgwick, the pioneer geologist, who was born in Dent in 1785.

Dent is a gem, with whitewashed houses crowded around narrow cobbled streets. It boasts two thoroughly traditional village pubs, one of which, The Sun, brews its very own Dent beer – and excellent beer it is, too. It is a place with a history. Once it was famous for its knitters – known as 'the terrible knitters of Dent', not for their poor skills, but for the furious speed at which they worked. Many local houses had knitting galleries attached, where the knitters sat and chatted to the accompaniment of a steely, rapid clicking of needles. In the nineteenth century, the marble industry was dominant, and examples can be seen as inlays in the floor of the fifteenth-century church **43**. Perhaps it was the presence of so many different rocks and stones that was the inspiration for Adam Sedgwick, a native of Dent who went on to become one of the pioneers of the new science of geology. His memorial **44** in the appropriate form of a slab of Shap granite stands near the entrance to the village.

Returning to Church Bridge, the walk continues along the riverbank and briefly joins the road. Almost immediately a stile leads back to the waterside path. The impressive high fells to the left encroach ever closer on the river, with rocky outcrops lending a hint of drama. Where the river swings away to the right, the path heads off towards the road and Barth Bridge **45**, which spans the river in a single arch. The changeable mood of the Dee is hinted at by four further arches, built to allow flood water an uninterrupted flow. Cross straight over the road and keep on the riverside path. The river itself seems to gather strength quite quickly, so that by now it is certainly more river than stream. It has a peaceful air, with woodland creeping up to the bank. The familiar dippers and wagtails are joined by chaffinches attracted by the trees. All the time the river is creeping closer to the steep hillside, forcing the path into a narrow obstacle course through a mass of tangled tree roots and stones. Across the river, the view is dominated by the shapely hill of Helms Knott. There is a small diversion away from the bank, across a footbridge, and the path is divided from the water by an old layered hedge before joining the road by a ford.

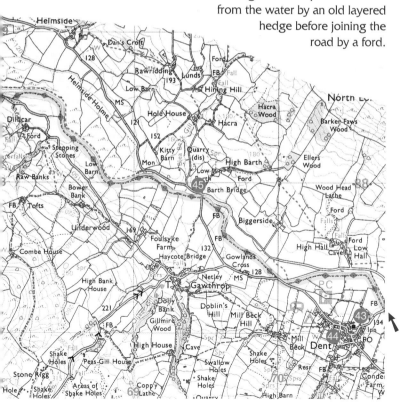

This remains a very pleasant walk, avoiding the river which has gone into convulsions, writhing across the fields. The delicate hues of meadow saxifrage peep out through the grass, together with the stronger shades of marsh marigolds and the brilliant white of wild garlic. The road goes gently but steadily uphill, past an area of mixed woodland, particularly attractive in spring when the bluebells are in flower. This road is scarcely more than a lane, running between traditional layered hedges which alternate with the more familiar stone walls. Brackens Gill comes down to the road through a parade of trees, with a sturdy farm at the edge. Across the water is a very grand house, Gate Manor,

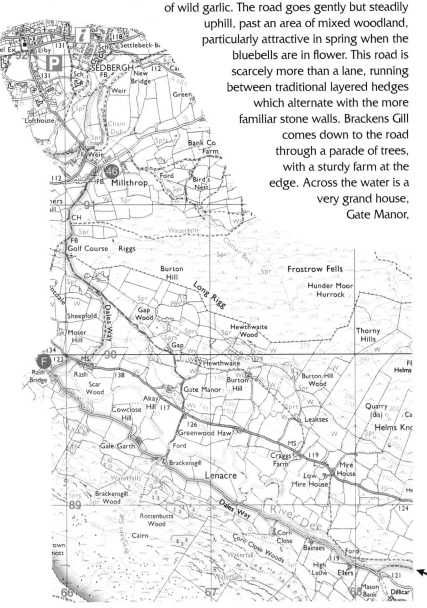

with a fine array of high chimneys standing proud above a complex of gables. A feature of this part of the walk is the preponderance of trees, which makes for a very rich, varied landscape. One could almost be walking through a sophisticated parkland designed by Capability Brown, but up ahead the rougher hills suggest that this will be a short-lived experience. After passing through an area of woodland with sycamore, beech and birch prominent, the road drops down to rejoin the river, which has expanded considerably even in such a short distance. Its dashing mountain nature has been tamed, and it now flows placidly between wide banks. This will, in fact, be the last encounter with the Dee, for the Way now turns right to cross Rash Bridge **F**. Looking downstream, one can see a weir across the river and the remains of a leat, which once took water away to power a mill.

Once across the bridge, turn right at the road junction, then left through the metal gate by the sign saying 'Footpath to Millthrop'. The path goes steeply uphill to a ladder stile at the top. Continue following the wall round to the left and cut across towards the patch of woodland. Great masses of stones can be seen piled up, having been here since the land was cleared. Some would have gone for wall-making, the rest have simply been left. Cross the stile at the uphill end of the copse – a small wood with a large bird population, chaffinch and the more elusive tree creeper both putting in an appearance. Follow the obvious footpath terraced into the hill by the wall. The view opens out towards the distant hills of the Lakeland fells beyond the foot of the valley. Take the broad track downhill towards Millthrop **46**. This most attractive village is much more typical of the Lake District than of the Dales, especially in the extensive use of slates. The Lakes still, however, lie some way ahead – this is just another effect of the geology of the Dent Fault. At the road junction turn left, then at the main road turn right to cross the bridge, an elegant structure with a sweeping curve. The route soon turns off the road, but many will want to carry on into Sedbergh for refreshment, a bed for the night or simply to explore. The broad main street is home to a market, behind which is an intriguing complex of alleys. Down one of these, Weavers Yard, is an old house with a massive chimney in which Bonnie Prince Charlie is said to have hidden after the disastrous rebellion of 1745. There is a classically styled grammar school of 1716 and an Early English church hiding under Victorian embellishments. It is a town of quiet prosperity, built largely on the woollen industry. The public school is some way out of town.

CIRCULAR WALK FROM DENT

5 ½ miles (9 km)

Starting at Church Bridge, Dent **A**, take the road up towards the village. Just beyond the house with an unusual weather vane showing a cat eyeing a mouse, turn right up the cobbled street, passing the Sedgwick stone **44**, and follow the main street past the Sun Inn. At the car park, turn left by the chapel **B**, taking the road marked as a dead end and signposted 'Bridleway to Flinter Gill'. Climb uphill past whitewashed cottages and the Zionist chapel, which has curious Gothic windows, not glazed but painted on the wall. The roadway runs out here and is replaced by a rough, stony track heading uphill to woodland. As the path climbs, so the large trees give way to the hardier hawthorn and birch. Gradually these too thin out to reveal meadows to the right, while to the left the gill has become a deep stone-lined gash in the land. The path comes very close to the stream, which plunges over high ledges in a waterfall **47**. At the top of the hill the stony track gives way to a grassy lane between stone walls. Turn left just beyond a wooden seat and a gate **C** where the path divides.

The path is now a broad green lane between stone walls. It crosses the stream that runs down into Flinter Gill and continues on a level round the shoulder of the hill. Down to the left there are splendid views into Dentdale while up ahead is the great hump of Whernside. After a mile and a half (2 km) this track ends at a T-junction **D** with another green lane, Nun House Outrake. Turn left to begin the walk back down to the valley. The descent is quite steep and can seem more like a scree slope than a footpath. The steepest section appears as the track bends round a small conifer plantation. The path crosses a stream by the farm and then becomes a surfaced track leading down to the road. Turn left at the road, passing an attractive house on the right with Gothic windows. The road goes downhill; just beyond an iron gate on the right, look for a wooden stile almost hidden in the hedge **E**.

Turn right across the stile and follow the line of the wall downhill. As the wall turns right continue across the field to the gate in the stone wall. Head across the next field towards the telegraph pole in the gap between the deciduous woodland and the conifers, to take the little path that winds down to the road at Mill Bridge **F**. Turn right at the road, then left over the ladder stile to join the Dales Way. Leaving the road, cross diagonally over the field and head for a prominent conifer, beyond which the stone wall leads down to a stile by the river. Turn right to follow the riverbank to the footbridge **G**. Cross the bridge and turn left along the opposite bank of the river. The walk continues along the riverside over a series of stiles to a point just beyond where two watercourses merge **H**. Turn right at the finger-post to cross the field to a wooden gate which opens into a narrow footpath, squeezed between stone wall and hedge. It leads down to the road. Turn left onto this typical Dentdale narrow country lane and head back to the bridge.

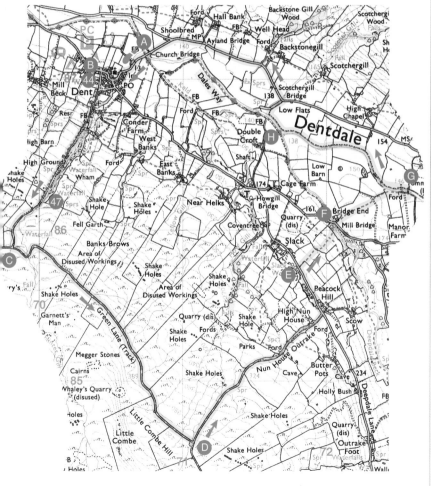

6 MILLTHROP TO BURNESIDE

via Brigflatts and the Crook of Lune   *15 miles (24 km)*

This section of the Way was characterised by a walker coming in the other direction as 'all gates and stiles'. It is difficult to disagree and, as a result, the following description might seem like a course in advanced orienteering. It is nowhere near as bad as it sounds, and the route is everywhere easy to follow. Moreover, the bald description gives no hint of the delights that lie ahead in a gentle countryside of river valleys and undulating hills, all immensely enjoyable but for the noisy intrusion of the motorway.

Once across the bridge from Millthrop, turn immediately left through a stone stile and an iron gate, onto the footpath signposted to Birks. Alongside the fence is the dried-up mill leat, and the mill itself **48** soon appears on the left. Cut across the middle of the field to a stile in the stone wall by the wood **A**. The path leads away to the right – rather a shame, as the path to the left, which eventually leaves the wood at the same point, runs high above the dashing River Rawthey. But whichever way is selected, this little wood has its share

Sedbergh seen against the background of high fells.

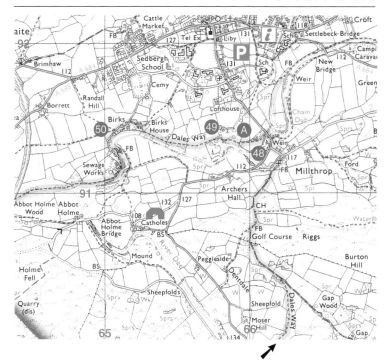

of curiosities. A deep trench lined with well-dressed stone runs through the middle, close by a small ruined archway. These are all that remain of grand Akay House, which once stood here, surrounded by parkland. On leaving the woods one passes one of the few surviving structures from the estate, a small folly tower **49**.

There are good views now of an almost perfectly conical hill over to the left, beyond which Dentdale stretches away. The path makes its way down to the river's edge beside a sports field. It passes a rather grand nineteenth-century house before going round the back of a little grassy knoll. At the roadway, turn left to return to the river, where another weir is followed by another mill **50**. Unlike the other mills around Sedbergh, which manufactured woollen yarn and cloth, this produced cotton. Once past the mill, take the stile on the left beside the river and the mill leat. A small gorge has been carved by the river galloping along at a good rate through the narrows. It soon opens out again as it arrives at the confluence with the Dee. There is now a pleasant walk over fields towards a high railway embankment. This is part of the disused line that once ran from Ingleton, and it will put in a few more appearances along the way.

The path goes up over the embankment and straight down the other side. Looking back, one has a good view of the single iron-arched viaduct that took the line across the river. A small weir now appears just before the river reaches Brigflatts. Once this hamlet was known only as a place where flax was spun to be woven into linen but, in 1652, George Fox came here to preach a new version of Christianity, which was to become known as Quakerism. Like other non-conformist creeds of the day, it was illegal, so the Friends of Sedbergh came to this lonely out-of-the-way spot to build their meeting house **51**. There is no direct access from the walk, except as a road detour, but it is a place of great charm: a cluster of seventeenth- and eighteenth-century whitewashed cottages.

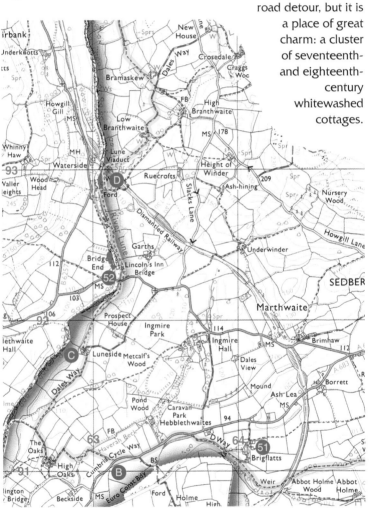

Beyond Brigflatts the riverbanks steepen but, as the river swings away to the left, the path comes straight on down to the road. Turn left, and a very grand house, Ingmire Hall, comes into view. Its sadly ruinous Gothic lodge now stands as an introduction not to the stately home but to a caravan park. The next turning is easily missed. The road turns round to the left, and the footpath sign is a fingerpost all but lost to view in the hedge **B** by a wooden stile; if you reach an iron fence then you have just missed it. Follow the path beside the hedge, cross a small stream and turn left to climb a small knoll before continuing along the ridge. At the hedge turn right, then left to go down a green lane towards the houses. At the end of the lane turn left then right through wooden gates, then turn right past Oaks Cottage and follow the lane that runs down between hedges. At the end of the lane, by a metal gate, turn right as indicated by a footpath sign to Lincoln's Inn Bridge. At the end of the field go through an iron gate to join a green lane, which is soon closed in by high hedges. At Luneside **C** continue round to an iron gate, where a helpful sign tells you exactly what to do – go across to the tree then follow the line of the fence. Watch out for a stile in the fence on the left – cross over here and continue in the same direction to reach the river and the sign for Lincoln's Inn Bridge **52**. Follow the road to the bridge itself. A circular walk starts here (see p. 122).

Turn right at the bridge, then left over the stile by the wooden gate and go straight on to the gate opposite. This is a pleasant stroll through meadows that are bright with summer flowers, while the River Lune alongside is quite dramatic, gushing down over a series of falls. Up ahead is another railway viaduct **D**, built in the same style as the last but altogether grander, with stone arches and a central iron span. In the fields the local farmer has surprisingly introduced Highland cattle, with their shaggy coats and long, sweeping horns. A stream cuts across the Way, presenting a choice. In dry weather it can easily be crossed at the ford but when it is swollen it may be necessary to make a detour, the directions for which are incorporated in the circular walk at the end of this section. The main walk takes the path under the viaduct arch by the yellow arrow to head diagonally up the hillside, then curves round the hill in the direction shown by the fingerpost. It is worth pausing to look back at the Lune Viaduct in its magnificent setting. At the top of the hill, head towards the iron gate and the obvious farm track. Up ahead is a great bowl formed by the Howgill Fells.

From Low Branthwaite, an attractive farm with a tall arched window in the centre of the façade, go straight across the access track to the ladder stile and the path signposted to Bramaskew. Head for the gap in the wall opposite, then turn left and follow the line of the hedge round to the metal gate on the left. Take the farm track, a narrow lane between stone walls. When you emerge from the lane, cut across the field towards a tree that is signposted 'Dales Way'. Once past the farm buildings, continue along the line of the hedge. This is all easy walking over meadows, with views out across the Lune valley. Pass below a small barn, cross the beck and join a lane running between high hedges. At the whitewashed farm with an impressive array of fine stone chimneys, turn left over a stile and follow the path to the right of the wall, then turn left to head downhill. The path goes past the farm buildings **E** to pass through the neat cobbled yard right in front of the house. One feels uncomfortably like an intruder but the moment soon passes. At the little wood, cross the footbridge and turn left to take the path back down to the river, and continue the walk along the bank.

The Lune here is a gurgling, busy river, home to a pair of oyster catchers. Cross a tributary stream on a footbridge and continue along the river's edge. The path now enters one of its squelchier phases, passing through an area of woodland which is more or less permanently running with water. The path wriggles through boulders and gnarled trees, and rises and falls with the undulations in the bank. There is no obvious route through the tangle, but to avoid the numerous bogs it is best to pick a way through the stones at the water's edge. This is easily done and adds a welcome touch of variety. It is soon possible to join an easier path below the low crags at the side. Where the way is closed off by a wire fence **F**, turn right up the rutted track and follow the path round the little hill and across the wide bend of the river – the Crook of Lune. Join the roadway and turn left over the bridge **53**.

It is with some reluctance that one leaves this most attractive river valley, since looming up ahead is the M6; the noise of motorway traffic will be an accompaniment for some time. Happily, however, there is much to enjoy closer at hand. First is the bridge itself, with its ragged stone arches and pleasing curved approach wall. The sense of moving away from the Dales towards the Lakes is reinforced by the pale-grey stone houses with their slate roofs. A small bridge leads over a romantic beck of waterfalls and tumbled rocks, each little waterfall ending in a dark pool worn out of the stone. There is also a last appearance of the Ingleton branch line, which crosses the valley on an 11-arch stone viaduct just before its junction with the main line. In fact, generations of transport systems meet here. Beneath the railway is a high-arched packhorse bridge, with the old road bridge behind it, while beyond that is the still-busy West Coast main line running alongside the latest addition, the M6.

Turn right at the first road junction, then left at the next, and then immediately left again onto the footpath by the stream which goes up past the oddly named Half Island House. At the top of this little lane continue to follow the line of the hedge up towards the brow of the hill.

There is an obvious route to follow through breaks in the hedges. On reaching a single tree, bear off to climb the hill towards the top corner of the field **G** and turn left on the farm approach road. The countryside is perfectly pleasant, but it is undeniably irritating to be walking along-side the M6 with its racket when all you really want to do is to get to the other side and leave it behind. Just before the farm, turn right over a somewhat makeshift stile and skirt round the farm wall to head off in the general direction of the line of telegraph poles. Cut across to a stile at the corner of the field to join the road, and turn left towards the sign-post opposite. Leave the road to follow the path along the side of the wall, then turn off onto the bridge across the motorway.

Once over the bridge turn immediately left to follow the road beside the motorway. Just beyond a rather dilapidated crash barrier, turn right through a metal gate then diagonally left to the stone stile and head down a little hollow towards the farm. Your back is now finally turned to the motorway. Take the broad track past Holme Park Farm. There is now an obvious path running in a straight line across the fields to join a lane bordered by hedges, which heads towards Morsedale Hall. Go round the back of the barns, cross the bridge over the stream, go up to the driveway gate and take the little path that runs steeply uphill towards a large copper beech. The path leads down to a driveway and crosses over to go through a small wood crowded with rhododen-drons. On leaving the wood, follow the fence down to a stile in the wall and turn left along the road, with a view of Grayrigg and its tall church tower over to the right.

Turn right at the road junction and left by the white house. Take the path beside the hedge down to the stiles and the busy main line. Cross the railway with care, remembering that it is used by trains travelling at a hundred miles an hour. This is, thankfully, the last major transport route to interrupt what has been and is now again a wholly delightful country walk.

The way ahead now offers an altogether pleasant prospect, a gentle swelling of green hills covered with gorse, as the path leads down to a little shaded brook. At the wall, turn left, then turn right onto the lane and follow it round towards the farm. Turn off between the bungalow and the farmhouse. Go along the surfaced track and, just before the cattle grid, turn right on the path beside the stream. Cross the stream, go through the farm buildings and take the track to the main road **H**. Turn right and almost immediately left onto the track heading to Thursgill Farm. There is a small refreshment stand here, which many will welcome. Having crossed over the stream, turn left over the gate and head for the stile opposite. This is very much a green-field walk across farmland, but no one could accuse it of monotony. Small fields create patterns that flow with the steady rise and fall of the land, and even the fields of long grass are never quite uniform. The wind can shake them so that they turn a silvery face to the light, and even on the stillest days they are flecked with meadow flowers. Carry on following the hedge up the hill, cross a stile and, where the hedge comes to an end, bear right towards a large white house. Just before the stone barn **I**, turn off to the left through a gate and carry on along a diagonal to the small clump of trees on a hummock, where the path curves gently round to a footbridge, a brief acquaintance with the busy River Mint.

Cross the river and head towards the gate. Turn right onto a stony track that swings round towards Shaw End **54**,

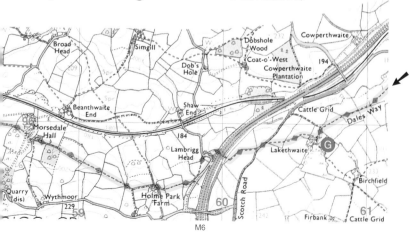

a particularly elegant house. Just before the clump of trees, turn left through a kissing gate to follow the broad track, and then turn left again between the houses. The Way goes in front of High Barn to join a narrow, overgrown lane. Cross straight over the minor road to take the surfaced track signposted to Biglands. Pass in front of the house to join a comfortable grassy track with fine views of the fells to the right. Head towards the pylon until you come to a stone stile in the corner of the field, and turn diagonally off to pass to the right of Black Moss Tarn. Now climb up the hill, still heading towards the pylon. One of the delights of this part of the walk is that every climb up every hill and rise seems to end in a view even better than the last. Go through the gate in front of New House Farm and take the path to the left of the house to follow a lane that runs between broken walls to join the surfaced track. The scenery offers a mixture of the very attractive and the downright ugly – a hillside of brilliant yellow gorse and a collapsed barn surrounded by rubble. The track goes steadily downhill between banks densely covered in cow parsley, but gradually the bank drops away to give a view of Kendal in the distance – the first glimpse of any large town since leaving Ilkley. The lane eventually runs down by a small wood to reach the busy A6 **J**.

Cross the main road and turn left then immediately right towards the farm. Go between the farm buildings, cross the yard and turn left through the wooden gate. Carry on to the second gate and follow the line of the hedge, taking the path around the bottom of the field to a large ladder stile in the corner. The path leads round a marshy area then goes right across a stile and a footbridge. Turn left to follow the line of the bridge. Ignore a metal gate on the right, and

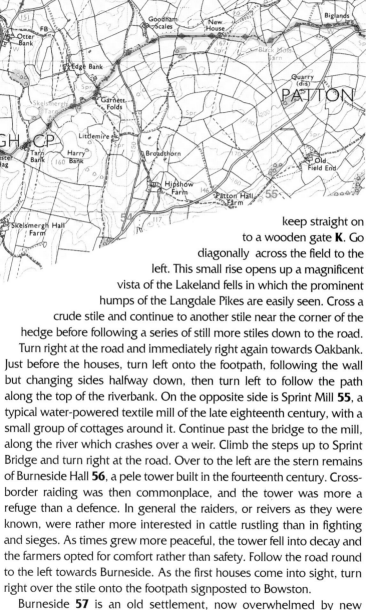

keep straight on to a wooden gate **K**. Go diagonally across the field to the left. This small rise opens up a magnificent vista of the Lakeland fells in which the prominent humps of the Langdale Pikes are easily seen. Cross a crude stile and continue to another stile near the corner of the hedge before following a series of still more stiles down to the road.

Turn right at the road and immediately right again towards Oakbank. Just before the houses, turn left onto the footpath, following the wall but changing sides halfway down, then turn left to follow the path along the top of the riverbank. On the opposite side is Sprint Mill **55**, a typical water-powered textile mill of the late eighteenth century, with a small group of cottages around it. Continue past the bridge to the mill, along the river which crashes over a weir. Climb the steps up to Sprint Bridge and turn right at the road. Over to the left are the stern remains of Burneside Hall **56**, a pele tower built in the fourteenth century. Cross-border raiding was then commonplace, and the tower was more a refuge than a defence. In general the raiders, or reivers as they were known, were rather more interested in cattle rustling than in fighting and sieges. As times grew more peaceful, the tower fell into decay and the farmers opted for comfort rather than safety. Follow the road round to the left towards Burneside. As the first houses come into sight, turn right over the stile onto the footpath signposted to Bowston.

Burneside **57** is an old settlement, now overwhelmed by new houses and the big paper mill which dominates the village. It is, however, a useful stopping place, offering shops, accommodation and a pub. It is also a short hop by bus or train to Kendal.

The Dales Way enjoys only a brief acquaintance with the busy and attractive River

Mint, which is crossed near Patton Bridge.

CIRCULAR WALK FROM LINCOLN'S INN BRIDGE

7 miles (11.5 km)

This walk incorporates an alternative route for the Dales Way to be used in wet weather. It starts at Lincoln's Inn Bridge **A**, following the Way along the riverbank towards the viaduct. At the wall **B**, where the stream is generally forded, turn right onto the path to be used when the stream is impassable. Head uphill and under the arch in the railway embankment. Go through a metal gate and turn left then right to follow the path beside the wall. This is a very peaceful little valley with meadows running down to the tree-shaded stream. At the head of the valley, footpaths meet at a signpost **C**. To resume the Dales Way, turn left to Low Branthwaite, but for the circular walk continue straight on along the track signposted to High Branthwaite. Go between the farm buildings, cross a stile and a stream and follow the wall to a wooden gate leading into a lane. Where the Dales Way meets the track **D** just before Bramaskew, turn right, up past the house to the road.

Turn left onto the road. Its straightness gives a clue to its origins: it was built in the first century AD to link the Roman fortress at Deva (modern Chester) with the northern frontier region. It runs along the bottom of the rough lower slopes of Howgill Fells, where curlews swoop and cry. Just before the turning to Thwaite **E**, bear left through the wooden gate by the signpost to Hole House. Continue to the gate opposite, cross the stile and turn left along the wall. Follow the stream and line of hawthorn to join the clear track down to Nether Bainbridge **F**. Turn right to join the Dales Way as it heads towards Hole House. The route now follows the Way down to the river and on to Crook of Lune Bridge **G**. (A full description of this section can be found on p. 114.)

Cross over the bridge and turn left onto the stone bridge that crosses the stream. Pass between two barns and then between the line of trees. Follow the track up beside the fence and, as you climb, you will find increasingly impressive views down to the river. At the top of the hill, join the farm track that goes through the railway arch to the road. Cross over to the double metal gates opposite to follow the track up beside the wall. It turns left above a quarry, then passes through a small grove of trees and swings round in a U-turn. Continue uphill, keeping a clump of trees on your right, then follow the line of the fence. Go through a metal gate and continue following the line of the wall. The path now

The seventeenth-century Quaker meeting house in the secluded hamlet of Brigflatts. It is still in use.

becomes a more distinct green lane, with vestiges of boundary walls to both sides. Follow the wall as it goes round to the left and, at the junction of the tracks **H**, go through the metal gate to the right and follow the wall to the iron gate. Turn left onto the road.

This is a peaceful open road with views over the fells; curlews appear to keep the walker company. The road climbs steadily as the landscape becomes rougher, with rocky outcrops thrusting through. The road passes a small Quaker graveyard, immediately beyond which is the massive rock of Fox's Pulpit **58**. It was here on Sunday 13 June 1652 that George Fox preached to a congregation of over a thousand, leading to the establishment of the Quaker meeting house at Brigflatts (see p. 112). From here continue on down the road, passing a bungalow, to the small settlement of New Field. Just before the first of the white-washed houses **I**, turn left onto a broad track that swings round to the right to a gate at the end of a stone wall. This part of the route is waymarked by yellow arrows. Cross over a small stream, follow the line of the wall, then take the track downhill beside the farm. There is now a delightful walk down a rich hillside meadow. Head over to the left to locate a stile at the edge of the wood and take the path that meanders off to the left through the trees and bracken to leave the wood again by a second stile. Still bearing left, follow the edge of the field and, as soon as the path begins to go uphill, cut across to a point slightly to the right of the line of trees on the left. Follow the line of hawthorn towards the metal gate at the road.

Cross over the road to the ladder stile almost lost in the hedge and carry straight on along the line of the hedge. There is another view now of the Lune Viaduct. Cross the stile to reach the road and turn left to cross Lincoln's Inn Bridge to return to the start.

7 BURNESIDE TO BOWNESS

via Cowen Head   *9 ½ miles (15 km)*

This is a short, final section, but one which provides a fitting climax to the whole walk. The path leaves the main road at Burneside, crosses a footbridge over a stream and follows the line of the hedge, with the paper mill on the far side. At the end of the field, turn left at the kissing gate and take the path down, not to the river as it might appear, but to the mill stream, beyond which is the actual River Kent, crossed by a large weir **59**. Having arrived at the riverside, the path promptly leaves it again. Follow the fence to a metal ladder stile and go straight on to rejoin the river, which runs between grassy banks overhung with trees. It may be possible to see a kingfisher here, a blue flash skimming the water.

At Bowston Bridge **A** cross the river and turn right at the road junction. Immediately beyond the turning to Kent Close, turn right onto the footpath. This is an unromantic stretch of river, flowing past a rubbish dump. The path leads to a minor roadway, with the river gurgling chirpily along beside it. The road is, in fact, laid on the trackbed of an industrial light railway that once linked the mills along the Kent with the Windermere branch line. There were two basic types of mill along the river, both relying on local coppiced woodland for raw material and the fast-flowing Kent for power: paper mills and bobbin mills. The latter used lathes and similar machines to turn the wooden bobbins used in the Lancashire cotton mills. The major mill complex appears at Cowen Head **60**, where a very impressive stone tower is surrounded by a little mill village of whitewashed cottages, followed, inevitably, by the weir. The mill has been converted into an attractive riverside development. Now the path becomes a gentle way through rolling pasture, leading down to the edge of the Kent. However, the scenery is changing, with more and more rocky outcrops giving a hard edge to the soft hills. The walk continues on the same bank, but cross the footbridge **B** for the circular walk (p. 136).

There follows a particularly delightful riverside walk, the water rushing and dashing over rocks, and the opposite bank shaded by majestic trees. The banks then begin to close in. The way is stony and the river goes down a natural staircase of ledges between a tumble of boulders. Then everything calms down, the path leading through an

The modern paper mill at Burneside.

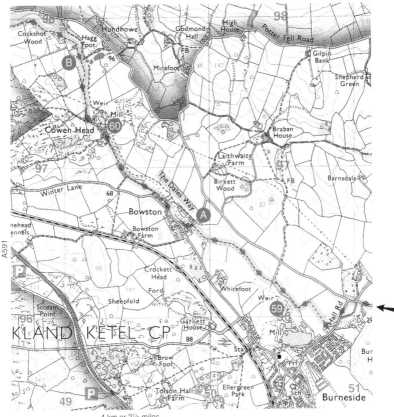

iron gate and across the field to a ladder stile. Cross the stile to go along the edge of a small copse of birch and oak. The Way now alternates between narrow, rocky tracks and comfortable strolls over smooth grassland. There is a hint of the grandeur that lies ahead in the hills across the river, their brows lined with crags. At the field separated from the river by a stone wall, head for the corner nearest the river and join the lane running between stone walls. Beyond the kissing gate, leave the broad riverside track to the left to go through a second kissing gate, and continue straight on in the direction shown by the footpath sign. Bear left down the path to the road and continue

Kendal, a popular stopover for walkers on the Dales Way, stands on the edge of the Lake District National Park.

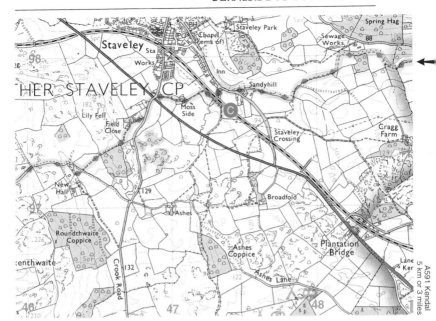

on the road by the river towards the outskirts of Staveley, an attractive spot mercifully released from holiday traffic by the bypass. Its main feature is the tower built in 1388, all that remains of St Margaret's church. A notice in the local pub recalls that in 1872 the Rev. Tom Bell caught a freshwater basking shark in the Kent. Special trains were run to view the 250 lb monster.

Just after the road reaches the river, turn left by Stockbridge Farm to take the track under the arch carrying the Windermere branch line **C**. Once through the arch, turn right onto the path beside the track, a little green lane running between drystone walls, and follow it round towards the white house. Cross the stile and, unlikely though it seems, go through the garden to the surfaced lane. Carry on down the lane to the road and turn left. Go straight over the busy main road and, once across the bridge, take the little slip road down to the right, passing a house with a splendid show of yew and cedar in the garden. The surfaced road peters out and the route continues as a green lane. Cross the field to the gate by the wood and follow the path alongside the edge of the woodland. Take the farm track to the road and turn right onto the minor gated road.

This is a quiet lane, offering en route a free roadside snack of blackberries in season. Here, perhaps for the first time, Lakeland is not so

Journey's end for walkers on the Dales Way: the lake shore at Bowness-on-Windermere.

much something to look forward to but a real presence. The road rises gently to a summit with an immense panorama of hills stretching from horizon to horizon, all the way from Howgill Fells to the Langdales and beyond. The lane now heads back downhill, shaded by trees, the banks and fields to either side bright with flowers, including the occasional orchid. The pattern of Lakeland fields is subtly different from that of the Dales. Here they are divided up into neat squares and rectangles, indicating later enclosure than the irregular fields in Dentdale and around Grassington. The land itself is also very different. Instead of a smooth-floored glacial valley, rising eventually to a rocky escarpment, there is an apparently random pattern of hummocks and hollows, with rock appearing on every side. Large piles of stone are left over from the days when this rugged land was cleared.

At the T-junction **D** turn right. Here is Fell Plain Farm, which is typical of the area. The house itself is, indeed, plain, but is rich in contrasting textures: walls are whitewashed, but window arches and door surrounds are left as natural stone, the whole being topped by a slate roof. The road goes steeply uphill; just as it begins to flatten out, turn left onto the bridleway running between stone walls. The path wanders through a rough, undulating landscape, with rocks showing on both sides. Just before the bridleway is crossed by a gate **E**, turn right through an iron gate in the wall. This is now wonderful walking country, with soft turf underfoot and great views all around. The path turns slightly away from the wall to avoid a patch of marshy ground. The outcrops invite one to sit down, not so much to rest as to enjoy the magnificent view.

The track now swings round to the right, past the conifers, way-marked by blue arrows on posts. At the end of the plantation, continue along the footpath by the stream, over a ladder stile and through a kissing gate to a field crowded with gorse bushes. Continue straight on round a marshy area, following a clear but sinuous track towards the corner of the stone walls, then turn right to cross a stile to join a farm track. At the top of the hill follow the track round in front of the farm, then turn off the track to the right to follow the line of the wall past a rocky knoll to the kissing gate in front of the stone house. Lakeland houses do not have dripstones over the windows, as in the Dales; here, protection is provided by a narrow stone course that juts out from the wall for the full length of the façade.

At the roadway **F** turn right and, as the road bends, turn left onto the track leading up through the farmyard to head for the gate

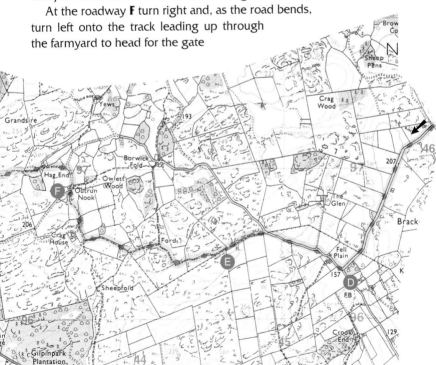

by the horse chestnut. Go through the avenue of trees, then turn right on the footpath by the wall. Cross a stone stile and go on up the little hill. From the crest one can see the obvious gate in the wall opposite. Skirt a small knoll, following a line just below the brow of the hill on the left until a waymark post comes into view. At the post, turn right. Now one can see the wooded slopes of Lake Windermere and the more distant Langdale Pikes. Once through a gap in the hedge by a waymark, turn left to the gate in the corner of the field. Turn left again to follow the farm track down by the wall. At the broad track **G**, turn sharply back to the left. (Anyone in a tearing hurry to get a train or bus can turn right for Windermere.)

The track runs through an area still surrounded by moorland and dotted with copses, passing oak, hawthorn and gorse. As the path goes downhill, so the coarse grass gives way to meadows increasingly rich with flowers. Eventually houses are reached; the first boasts some fine ornamental trees, a copper beech and a blazing variety of rhododendrons. The track now becomes a surfaced road serving the various houses along the way, passing a small tarn on the left with its resident swans. Turn right onto the road, which can be busy in summer. It runs up to the edge of Windermere Golf Course. Just beyond this, by a bunker, turn right down what appears at first glance to be a private driveway to a rather grand house. But almost immediately the drive forks and the route goes to the left, as indicated by a yellow arrow **H**. The track is shaded by a variety of rich, scented conifers.

Just before reaching an attractive whitewashed farmhouse, turn left onto a rough track leading to a wooden gate. Turn right at the gate to follow the path down by the garden wall. Continue following the path through three kissing gates, then turn off on a diagonal to the right towards the wooden post on the brow of the hill. Carry on through the gap in the trees that line up along this little knoll. As you approach the brow, a second wooden post confirms the direction. Head for the gate in the stone wall and continue crossing a rocky, lumpy landscape, making for the left side of a prominent stony outcrop. Cross straight over the road via two kissing gates and follow the path down beside the hedge. Cross the next roadway and go through the kissing gate. Where the path forks **I**, go left round the edge of a small patch of woodland. Leaving the wood behind, go through the gate and turn right onto a driveway then immediately left to follow the footpath beside the iron fence. Go through an iron gate, then continue in the same direction to the far corner of the field.

Go through an iron gate and follow the path beside the wall. Cross the farm approach road to take the path between stone walls – at the

gate you get your first
glimpse of the waters of Windermere.

Continue on down the field, crossing over the track that
heads to an area of mature woodland. The path leads down towards
the houses, a stone seat **61** giving a magnificent view over
Windermere and the fells beyond. It is there, as a plaque announces,
'For those who walk the Dales Way'. And here the walk officially
ends. But, of course, the walking is not quite over. There is still a final
stretch down into Bowness itself, with its milling holiday crowds, a
startling contrast to the loneliness of so much of the Dales Way. It can
seem an anticlimax, so perhaps the best solution is to march resolutely on to the water's edge, sit by the lakeside and look out over
the Cumbrian hills – perhaps finding inspiration for the next walk. It
will need to be a good one to match the delights of the Dales Way.

At the end of a long walk the sights of Lake Windermere can be enjoyed in style

...aboard one of the old pleasure craft.

Circular walk from Hagg Foot

4 ½ miles (7 km)

The walk begins by crossing the footbridge **A** upstream of Cowen Head and following the path up to the farm at Hagg Foot. Turn left at the road and after a little way turn right up stone steps to a stile by a signpost marking the footpath to Frost Hole **B**. Go diagonally uphill to the left of a small rock outcrop and, as you come over the brow of the hill, head for the uphill end of the continuous line of woodland and go through the metal gate between the wood and the copse. Over to the left is a stream and a small waterfall. The route now follows a very rough, stony track, going steadily uphill, and one can see how, wherever possible, naturally placed rocks have been incorporated into the wall to save labour. Coming out from under the cover of the trees that line the stream, turn sharp right just before a gate with a stern 'No Right of Way, No Footpath' sign.

Take the somewhat indistinct path in the direction shown by the Potter Tarn sign **C**, passing between two patches of hawthorn. At the brow of the hill, go through a gap in the stone wall on the right and follow the line of the wall on the left. Go through another gap in the wall to head slightly to the left of the little hill, when Potter Tarn **62** will come into view. Follow the edge of the tarn round to pass in front of the dam, and head for the stile in the wall to the left. Continue along the fairly clear track that runs along a little bank, crossing a stream by a small waterfall and continuing on the grassy track through the bracken. The cheerful if monotonous song of the meadow pipit may be heard at this point. At the top of the hill, cross the ladder stile and head off through the heather to a second tarn which now comes into view.

The next expanse of water, Gurnal Dubs **63**, has also been dammed to create a reservoir. Cross the dam wall; the local population of black-headed gulls seem not to welcome intruders and set up a noisy protest chorus. The track now turns away from the lake to head off again through the heather and joins another stony track **D**. Turn right past a marshy area of sphagnum and cotton grass. The path swings to the left, offering views out over Kendal and the surrounding high fells. The next turning is not signposted so a little mental arithmetic is called for. After the path turns left, two stone walls come in on the left-hand side. Now start counting the walls on the right: at the fourth, where the road dips downhill, go through the metal gate on the right **E**. Continue straight down the hill, following the line of the wall. At the rocky outcrop near the bottom, turn right to head for the metal gate that leads onto the road **F**.

Turn right again into this very quiet lane, which runs between stone walls, the verges brightened by hawthorn and gorse. The road turns downhill, overshadowed by fine oak and birch, which are home to a rowdy rookery. At the bottom of the hill is Godmond Hall **G**. Immediately beyond the garden, turn right by the Public Footpath sign and bear diagonally left across the field, aiming for the end of a line of trees. Cross over the lane and the stone stile opposite and turn right onto the path through the woods beside the little stream. Cross the stream on the footbridge and turn diagonally right towards the farm buildings. Join the surfaced track on the right to go past the buildings and through the iron gate to the green lane beside the stream. Where the path swings away, turn left through the wooden gate and you come to a sign marking the bridleway to Hundhowe. From here follow the farm access track down to the road **H** and turn right to return to the start.

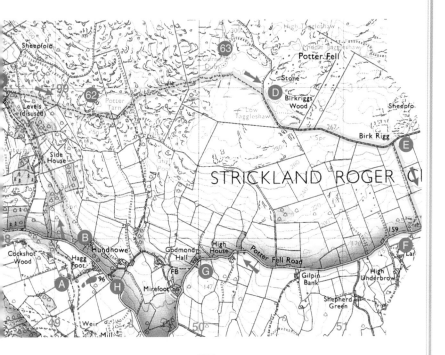

USEFUL
INFORMATION

Transport

Information on transport to and from the Dales Way is given in *The Dales Way Handbook*, published annually by the West Riding Area of the Ramblers' Association and the Dales Way Association (obtainable from them at their addresses on pages 141 and 142). This includes information on trains, buses and taxis, long-stay parking and self-drive cars for hire. There is also a useful publication on buses, available from local Tourist Information Centres and National Park Information Centres, called *Dales Connections*.

Trains from Windermere connect at Oxenholme with trains to London Euston. There is a frequent bus service between Bowness and Windermere during the summer months, though this is less frequent out of season. Buses to the start of the walk are available from Leeds Central Bus Station.

Accommodation

The Dales Way Handbook (see *Transport*) includes information on camp sites, bunkhouse barns and bed and breakfast accommodation. The following youth hostels are on or near the Dales Way at:

GR 970724   Whernside House, Kettlewell BD23 5QU (tel. 01756 760232)

GR 773851   Cowgill, Dent, Sedbergh LA10 5RN (tel. 01539 625251)

GR 515924   Highgate, Kendal LA9 4HE (tel. 01539 724066)

GR 405013   High Cross, Bridge Lane, Troutbeck, Windermere LA23 1LA (tel. 01539 443543)

GR 998627   The Old Rectory, Linton-in-Craven, Skipton BD23 5HH (tel. 01756 752400)

Details of opening times should be checked with the YHA Accommodation Guide or with the Northern Regional Office, P O Box 11, Matlock, Derbyshire DE4 2XA (sel. 01629 825850)

Bunkhouse barns are at: Barden Tower (GR 050572), Hubberholme (GR 929780), Cam Houses (GR 824822), Ribblehead – Station Inn (GR 765791) and Catholes (GR 653908).

Information about bed and breakfast accommodation can be obtained from Tourist Information Centres and from Stilwell's *National Trail Companion.*

TOURIST INFORMATION CENTRES

Cumbria Tourist Board   Ashleigh, Holly Road, Windermere LA23 2AQ (tel. 01539 444444)
Yorkshire Tourist Board   312 Tadcaster Road, York YO2 2HF (tel. 01904 707961)

Bowness-on-Windermere   Glebe Road, Bowness-on-Windermere LA23 3HJ (tel. 01539 442895)
Grassington   National Park Centre, Hebden Road, Grassington BD23 5LB (tel. 01756 752774)
Ilkley   Station Road, Ilkley, LS29 8HA (tel. 01943 602319)
Kendal   Town Hall, Highgate, Kendal LA9 4DL (tel. 01539 725758)
Leeds   The Railway Station, Leeds, LS1 1PL (tel. 0113 242 5242)
Otley   Council Offices, 8 Boroughgate, Otley, LS21 3AH (tel. 0113 247 7707)
Sedbergh   72 Main Street, Sedbergh LA10 5BL (tel. 01539 620125)
Windermere   Victoria Street, Windermere LA23 1AD (tel. 01539 446499)

USEFUL ADDRESSES

British Trust for Ornithology, Beech Grove, Tring, Hertfordshire HP12 5NR
The Countryside Commission
   Northern: Warwick House, Grantham Road, Newcastle upon Tyne NE2 1QF (tel. 0191 2328252)
   Yorkshire and the Humber: 2nd Floor, Victoria Wharf, Embankment 4, Sovereign Street, Leeds LS1 4BA (tel. 0113 246 9222)
Cumbria Wildlife Trust, Brockhole, Windermere LA23 1LJ (tel. 01539 432476)
The Dales Way Association, David Smith, Hon. Membership Secretary, Dalegarth, Moorfield Road, Ilkley, West Yorkshire LS29 8BL. The Association is a voluntary organisation which keeps the paths of the Way properly maintained and waymarked. They are constantly looking for improvements in the route and it is always worth checking the *Dales Way Handbook* for the most recent changes.

English Nature

    Cumbria: Juniper House, Murley Ross, Oxenholme Road, Kendal LA9 7RL (tel. 01539 792800)

    Yorkshire: The Institute for Applied Biology, University of York, York YO1 5DD (tel. 01904 432700)

Friends of the Lake District, No. 3, Yard 77, Highgate, Kendal, Cumbria LA9 4ED

Lake District National Park, Brockhole National Park Centre, Windermere, Cumbria LA23 1JL (tel. 01539 446601)

Ordnance Survey, Romsey Road, Maybush, Southampton SO9 4DH

Ramblers' Association, 1-5 Wandsworth Road, London SW8 2XX (tel. 0171 582 6878)

Royal Society for Nature Conservation, The Green, Witham Park, Waterside South, Lincoln LN5 7JR (tel. 01522 544400)

Royal Society for the Protection of Birds, The Lodge, Sandy, Bedfordshire SG19 2DL

Yorkshire Dales Society, Civic Centre, Cross Green, Otley, West Yorkshire LS21 1HD

Yorkshire Dales National Park Information Services, Colvend, Hebden Road, Grassington via Skipton, North Yorkshire BD23 5LB (tel. 01756 752748)

Yorkshire Wildlife Trust, 10 Toft Green, York YO1 1JT (tel. 01904 659570)

Youth Hostels Association, Trevelyan House, 8 St Stephens Hill, St Albans, Hertfordshire AL1 2DY (tel. 01727 855215)

Ordnance Survey maps covering the Dales Way

Landranger Maps (scale 1:50 000) 97, 98, 104
Explorer Maps (scale 1:25 000) 26 Nidderdale
                                      27 Lower Wharfedale and Washburn Valley

Pathfinder Maps
(scale 1:25 000)
683 Leeds
672 Harewood
671 Keighley and Ilkley
662 Bolton Abbey
617 Sedbergh
628 Kirkby Lonsdale

Outdoor Leisure Maps
(scale 1:25 000)
The Yorkshire Dales Southern (10)
The Yorkshire Dales Northern and Central (30)
The Yorkshire Dales Western (2)
The Lake District (7)

BIBLIOGRAPHY

Abbott, Stan and Whitehouse, Alan, *The Line That Refused to Die*, Leading Edge, 1990

Burton, Anthony, *Ordnance Survey Landranger Guide Book: The Yorkshire Dales and York*, OS/Jarrold, 1989

Garner, Lawrence, *Drystone Walls*, Shire Publications, 1984

Hartley, Marie and Ingilby, Joan, *The Yorkshire Dales*, Smith Settle, 1991

— *The Old Hand Knitters of the Dales*, Dalesman, 1991

— *The Yorkshire Dales*, Smith Settle, 1991

— *Life and Tradition in the Yorkshire Dales*, Dalesman, 1991

Ordnance Survey Leisure Guide: Yorkshire Dales, AA/Ordnance Survey, 1987

Raistrick, Arthur, *Buildings in the Yorkshire Dales*, Dalesman, 1981

— *Lead Mining in the Mid-Pennines*, D. Bradford Barton, 1973

— *The Pennine Walls*, Dalesman, 1981

Ramblers' Association/West Riding Area Dales Way Association, *Dales Way Handbook* (published annually)

Waltham, Tony, *The Yorkshire Dales National Park*, Webb & Bower/Michael Joseph, 1987

Wright, Geoffrey, *Roads and Trackways of the Yorkshire Dales*, Moorland, 1985

PLACES TO VISIT
ON OR NEAR THE DALES WAY

Armley Mills, Canal Road, Armley, Leeds
Kirkstall Abbey and Abbey House Museum, Kirkstall, Leeds
Leeds
    Leeds City Art Gallery, The Headrow
    Leeds City Museum, Municipal Buildings
    Royal Armouries Museum, Crown Point Road
    Tetley's Brewery Wharf, The Waterfront
    Tropical World, Canal Gardens, Roundhay Park
    Thackeray Medical Museum, St James' Hospital, Beckett Street
Manor House Museum and Art Gallery, Castle Yard, Ilkley
Embsay Steam Railway, Embsay
Bolton Priory
Barden Tower
Parcevall Hall Gardens, Skyreholme
National Park Centre, Colvend, Hebden Road, Grassington
Upper Wharfedale Museum, Main Street, Grassington

Dent Brewery,
National Park Centre, 72 Main Street, Sedbergh
Friends' Meeting House, Brigflatts
Holme Farm, Sedbergh
Abbot Hall Art Gallery, Kirkland, Kendal
Abbot Hall Museum of Lakeland Life and Industry, Kirkland, Kendal
Kendal Museum, Station Road, Kendal
Windermere Steamboat Museum, Rayrigg Road, Windermere
Lake District National Park Visitor Centre, Brockhole, Windermere